ELLIS WATERHOUSE

ITALIAN
BAROQUE PAINTING

ITALIAN
BAROQUE PAINTING

BY
ELLIS WATERHOUSE

WITH 198 ILLUSTRATIONS

PHAIDON

© 1962 PHAIDON PRESS LTD · 5 CROMWELL PLACE · LONDON SW7
FIRST PUBLISHED 1962
SECOND EDITION 1969

PHAIDON PUBLISHERS INC · NEW YORK
DISTRIBUTORS IN THE UNITED STATES · FREDERICK A. PRAEGER INC
111 FOURTH AVENUE · NEW YORK · N.Y. 10003
LIBRARY OF CONGRESS CATALOG CARD NUMBER: 69-12793

SBN 7148 1366 4 (CLOTH)
SBN 7148 1367 2 (PAPER)

MADE IN GREAT BRITAIN
PRINTED BY ROBERT MACLEHOSE AND CO LTD · UNIVERSITY PRESS · GLASGOW

CONTENTS

To
Cecil Gould
and
Michael Levey

PREFACE

THERE are no footnotes in this book, because it is meant to be that kind of book. It is addressed to readers who like to *look* at pictures for the pleasure they give, and who may have some difficulty in finding their way through a period from which so many acres of dingy canvas or depressing fresco have survived. I have looked again during the last few years at the works of all the painters mentioned in this book, and I have tried to choose for comment those works which have given me the greatest pleasure—and also those which are visible, either from accessibility or an absence of grime. Only a few works have been put in as a necessary concession to the history of art, and only a very few painters have been mentioned whose work has not seemed worth illustrating. This is not a book designed in any way for those who may have to pass an examination in the subject, but I have taken a good deal of trouble to date the works discussed as accurately as possible.

It is here that the absence of footnotes induces a feeling of guilt. When I have taken an idea from some other scholar I have mentioned his name, but to list every book or article to which I have been indebted for a date or a fact, would have meant a very long appendix. I hope the very many writers to whom I am indebted will forgive me. My greatest debt is to all those who have been responsible for collecting and cataloguing the splendid series of Exhibitions of seventeenth-century painting in Italy, notably at Bologna, in the years since the war. It is these Exhibitions alone which have made a book like the present one possible. I am also much beholden to Michael Levey and John Woodward, who have perused my manuscript.

E.K.W.

PRECURSORS OF THE BAROQUE AGE

LEADERSHIP in the arts within the frontiers of Italy has been less fixed in one centre than in any other Western country. In the second half of the sixteenth century Venice was the great creative centre for the art of painting, where the confident art of the High Renaissance, tinged only superficially, in the person of Tintoretto, with some of the evasiveness of Mannerism, lingered on in a St. Martin's summer. The great Venetian painters died off in the twenty years following 1575: Titian in 1576, Veronese in 1588, Jacopo Bassano in 1592, and Tintoretto in 1594. At almost the exact moment of Tintoretto's death the creative centre moved to Rome, which became the metropolis for the patronage of the arts in which painters and architects from North and Central Italy attained maturity. The two complementary sister styles of the seventeenth century, Baroque and Classicism, were evolved in Rome between about 1595 and 1625. They reached their first definitive statement in the work of Pietro da Cortona and of Poussin in the 1630's. To the generation of painters who preceded this unequivocal manifestation of the Baroque, and who laid the seeds of Poussin's Classicism, it is convenient, but not wholly illuminating, to give the name 'Proto-Baroque'. The great figures of this period are Caravaggio, Annibale Carracci, Domenichino, Lanfranco, and the first phases of Guido Reni and Guercino. But one does not introduce the painting of seventeenth-century Italy altogether correctly just by gracefully acknowledging the close of the great Venetian tradition of the High Renaissance and moving on to this next generation of great names, all of whom owed so much, in one way or another, to Venice. There were two painters who certainly do not belong to the Renaissance, and whose work fits with difficulty into the fairly consistent style of the group of Proto-Baroque painters, yet who were profoundly influential for seventeenth-century painting, especially outside Rome. One was a great artist in his own right, Federico Barocci: the other, Cesari d'Arpino, was conceived by conservative taste to be the greatest master in Rome in the middle 1590's, and his early work left a profound imprint on the leaders of the Lombard school, who were training in Rome during those years.

Federico Barocci (1535?–1612), after a brief and unhappy experience working in Rome 1561/63, at the Casino di Pio IV, spent the rest of his life in the enjoyment of ill health at his native Urbino. Though the town was remote, the Ducal collection was rich in masterpieces by the young Raphael and by Titian, and Baroccio had studied the frescoes in the Vatican in his youth. He seems also to have absorbed, in a manner not fully explained, a good deal of the spirit of Correggio. He was a tireless and beautiful draughtsman from the living model, and his naturally devout and perhaps simple and uncomplicated temperament invests his great series of altar-

1. BAROCCIO: *The Circumcision*. Paris, Louvre

pieces with a sincerity of feeling, which is woefully lacking in the work of such Mannerist contemporaries as, say, Giorgio Vasari. He was also a born painter with a feeling for tone and a liking for pretty colour. The Louvre *Circumcision* (fig. 1) of 1590 shines out in a room of Mannerist and Proto-Baroque pictures with a lyrical sweetness which never fails to astonish—but this is not all. The figures move in a great airy hall, which is the furthest possible removed from the unreality of Mannerist space conventions: the swirling, spiral design is an invention of genius: and the still life in the lower right-hand corner is almost worthy of Chardin. It is not

2. BAROCCIO: *The Visitation*. Rome, Chiesa Nuova

surprising that Baroccio received commissions for altarpieces from as widely scattered places as Genoa, Tuscany and Rome, and that wherever they were set up they influenced the local painters. His altarpieces were almost alone in satisfying the needs of the more serious but less sophisticated wing of the Counter-Reformation. The *Visitation* (Rome, Chiesa Nuova; fig.2), which had been commissioned by the Fathers of the Oratory in 1583 and was set up in 1586, is the one picture known to have been intensely admired by S. Filippo Neri, who was found on one occasion in ecstasy in front of it. Twenty years later Caravaggio was to produce religious

3. CESARI D'ARPINO: Detail from the frescoes in the Church of S.Prassede, Rome

pictures of the same deeply felt simplicity, one of them for the same Church. There is no stylistic link between the art of Baroccio and that of Caravaggio, but the spiritual link, which may with much probability be found in the work of the Oratory, is important for understanding the new religious painting which was to lead on towards the Baroque.

Giuseppe Cesari, known as the Cavaliere d'Arpino (1568–1640), is the Roman painter whose work was most highly prized, especially for frescoes and large schemes of decoration, by Clement VIII and Paul V during the years of the Proto-Baroque. The extreme dullness and backwardness of the work of his last forty years has obscured the real promise and originality he showed, about 1592, when he frescoed the ceiling of the Olgiati Chapel in Sta Prassede (fig.3). These richly and boldly coloured figures were different from the pale wraiths of so much Mannerist decoration: they cast shadows and have volume: and the grand style of the Roman High Renaissance is recalled. The Moses is unashamedly Michelangelo's, but without the muscle-bound air which obsessed Michelangelo's closer imitators. The style shows an escape from Mannerism along the same lines, but with enormously less intellectual distinction, as Annibale Carracci's solution, which he was to bring to Rome a year or two later. For a brief moment the false dawn seemed to be the real one, and, in 1593, when the Senators and Magistracy of Rome were looking for 'an exquisite, superlative, altogether excellent, unique, rare and reputed painter' (to translate the fulsome Latin of the document) to paint frescoes from Roman history on the walls of the main hall of the Capitoline Palace, their choice fell upon Arpino. These were still unfinished by 1608 and their style was then out of date, but the best parts of them have perhaps been undervalued.

Arpino may have been working at the Olgiati Chapel during the few months that Caravaggio was an assistant in his studio. The young Lombard painters, Cerano and Morazzone, whose student years in Rome fell at this moment were profoundly impressed by this phase of Arpino and returned to Milan before something newer had taken its place. In Naples too Arpino's frescoes of the 1590's on the ceiling of the nave and in the Sacristy of S. Martino are more distinguished than anything which had been painted there for fifty years. But at Naples, as at Rome, he was to be eclipsed almost at once by Caravaggio.

ROME: HISTORICAL NOTE

ROME recovered slowly from its Sack by the Imperial troops in 1527 and the central concern of the Papacy during the middle of the century was the problem of Reform, which was worked out at the Council of Trent, which lasted from 1545 to 1563. The beginning—and the peak period—of the Counter-Reformation was during the rule of Paul IV (Caraffa) from 1555 to 1559. Confidence gradually returned during the next decades and an atmosphere of greater relaxation, in which art patronage on a grand scale again became possible in Rome, had set in by 1592, when Clement VIII was elected Pope. It is with him that a new age began for Rome, in which she was once again the centre of Italian art. His own taste was extremely conservative, but some of his Cardinals led the way in the new patronage. The force which made Rome the great centre of painting, sculpture and architecture in Italy—and the Mecca for the artists of the rest of Europe—during the next hundred years, was the patronage of Popes and Cardinals and of the princely members of their families, and a list of the Popes, with their family names, will make the reading of the story easier.

Clement VIII (Aldobrandini) 1592–1605	Clement IX (Rospigliosi) 1667–1669
Paul V (Borghese) 1605–1621	Clement X (Altieri) 1670–1676
Gregory XV (Ludovisi) 1621–1623	Innocent XI (Odescalchi) 1676–1689
Urban VIII (Barberini) 1623–1644	Alexander VIII (Ottoboni) 1689–1691
Innocent X (Pamphily) 1644–1655	Innocent XII (Pignatelli) 1691–1700
Alexander VII (Chigi) 1655–1667	Clement XI (Albani) 1700–1721

1 : ANNIBALE CARRACCI AND HIS PUPILS

THERE is something beautifully apposite in the fact that, in 1595, the year after Tintoretto's death, Annibale Carracci should have been summoned to Rome to paint in the Farnese Palace, and to transfer, as it turned out, the creative centre of Italian painting from Venice to Rome. Without Rome, and the daily experience of Raphael and the Antique, he could never have achieved the final perfection of his mature style: and without a commission of an altogether exceptional kind, he would have had no opportunity to show the wonderful powers of which he was capable; for the Galleria Farnese, both in its ceiling and in the decoration of the entrance wall, has still claims to be considered one of the half dozen most beautiful rooms in the world—even though inferior busts have replaced the classical statues which once adorned the niches.

The Villa Farnesina, on the opposite side of the river from the Palazzo Farnese, where Raphael had designed for Agostino Chigi the *Story of Psyche* on the ceiling of a room of no great size, had passed to the Farnese in 1580. The rooms in the family Palace which looked over the river towards the Villa were still undecorated, when the young Cardinal Odoardo Farnese (1573–1626: created Cardinal 1591) took up his residence there and set about adorning the rooms in which he was to live himself and display the classical marbles that he had inherited from his great-uncle, Cardinal Alessandro Farnese (d. 1589), who had been the creator of Caprarola and one of the greatest patrons of art of his age. He also had the use of the Farnesina and the advice of Fulvio Orsini (1529–1600), who had been his great-uncle's librarian, and was for a time his own tutor. Orsini was one of the most eminent antiquarians of his time and his own classical collections, which were kept in the Palazzo Farnese, were to be bequeathed to Cardinal Odoardo. These conditions probably account for the fact that, at a time when the Counter-Reformation had by no means spent itself, a Prince of the Church could revive the practice of adorning his rooms with frescoes of scenes drawn from classical mythology. The Galleria was to be a sort of complement to the *Sala di Psiche* in the Farnesina and the room was to be used to display some of the most prized classical marbles from the Farnese collection. It has been shown by J. R. Martin that Fulvio Orsini was responsible for the programme of the *Camerino*, a small room which Annibale decorated 1595/97 as a first task, while feeling his way towards the design for the larger *Galleria*—and there seems little reason to doubt that Orsini was also responsible for the elaborate programme of the *Galleria* also, which showed the Power of Love as exemplified in a curious selection of incidents from classical mythology. The precedents which Annibale was bound to study for this were Raphael's frescoes and the Sistine ceiling, and, for the figure style, classical sculptures: and it is from the intensive study of these three sources, on top of the wide culture from Venetian and North Italian painting that he had acquired during his years at Bologna (see pp. 85–87), that Annibale perfected his final, classic, style. The Galleria Farnese and the considerable number of easel pictures which Annibale produced between 1595 and 1605, when his health gave out, were to be the most influential models for the whole of Roman Seicento painting. Annibale laid down the lines from which Baroque ceiling decoration was to develop, and he set the tone for seventeenth-century Classicism and created the 'classical landscape'.

The Galleria Farnese is not a room of great size. It measures about 68 × 21 feet, and is about 32 feet high (fig.4). The main cove of the ceiling was executed between 1597 and 1600 and is the work of Annibale, except for the two scenes in the centres of the side-slopes (*Cephalus and Aurora* and *The Triumph of Galatea*), which are by his brother Agostino, who was in Rome 1597–1599. In the decoration of the end walls and the entrance wall, Annibale was considerably helped by assistants, including Domenichino, who arrived in Rome in 1602: these seem to have been

4. ANNIBALE CARRACCI: The Galleria Farnese, Rome

completed about 1608. The figure scale is beautifully calculated to the size of the
room (and no doubt to the statues which once adorned the niches): the flesh tone is
of a natural healthy rose, which makes a striking contrast to the marbles and the
white *stucchi finti* which frame the side panels and are startlingly realistic. The
combination of these last with flesh-coloured Nudes and Putti, supporting bronze-
green circular reliefs, framed in white (fig.5), is of the greatest elegance. The main
scenes are all framed as if they were easel pictures—the central scene in white and
the two octagons and two central scenes on the curves in gold—and the appearance
of patches of sky at the angles at each end suggests that the whole arrangement is
that of a sort of booth at a picture fair in the open air. This ingenious angle treatment was to be of great importance for the later development of Baroque ceilings.
The blue of the sky picks up the only strong colour in the main subjects, the blue of
Ariadne's dress in the central *Triumph of Bacchus and Ariadne* (fig.6), a splendid
composition which seems to belong to the same world as Raphael's *Galatea* in the
Farnesina. A problem which was to haunt Baroque ceiling decoration is that a
ceiling can never look the right way round from all points. Annibale's compromise
is to make it look most the right way round from the entrance door (which has only
a window wall opposite to it) and to elaborate the wall treatment on the entrance and

5. ANNIBALE CARRACCI: Detail from the Galleria Farnese

6. ANNIBALE CARRACCI: *The Triumph of Bacchus*. Rome, Galleria Farnese

7. ANNIBALE CARRACCI: *Domine, quo vadis?*
London, National Gallery

end walls, so that the eye is mainly occupied with them from the other principal points of view. This multiple interest is not a Baroque feature, and the next generation of Roman ceiling decorators concentrated on an overwhelming single impression.

Although the single subjects are all excellent examples of Annibale's classic style, the character of this new style can be grasped in a more concentrated form in some of the smaller pictures he was painting during his Roman years, of which the most remarkable is perhaps the *Domine, quo vadis?* in the National Gallery, London (fig.7). This small panel has the monumentality of classical sculpture and the forms have a corresponding solidity: but they are animated by a dramatic tension and express the passions of modern man with a calculated nicety of rhetorical gesture and expression. Raphael's Cartoons were the great models for this new language, which is as remote from the ambiguities of Mannerism as the pictures of Caravaggio, but bespeaks a much greater intellectual energy than is ever to be found in Caravaggio. The hundreds of splendid drawings which have survived for the Galleria Farnese and most of Annibale's other works help us to appreciate the nature of his genius. He commands our respect both for his infinitely painstaking study of nature and for the brainwork with which he refined his finished designs. As a naturalistic draughtsman he has hardly been surpassed.

The figures in the *Domine, quo vadis?* are not seen in isolation. They are set against a landscape which has been studied, selected, and idealized so as to be a perfect foil for them. This creation of the 'classical landscape' setting, although it owes much to Venetian precedent, was Annibale's own creation. With a reduction in the size of the figures, Landscape—which had hitherto in Rome been a monopoly of Flemish artists, such as the Brill brothers—comes into its own as a new genre in Italian painting. Annibale had experimented with landscape of a looser and more picturesque kind during his years at Bologna, but the great examples of his Roman years are the series of lunettes, with sacred subjects for staffage, which were painted by Annibale and his pupils (Domenichino and Albano) between 1600 and 1604 for the Chapel of the Palazzo Aldobrandini and are now in the Doria-Pamphily Gallery

8. ANNIBALE CARRACCI: *The Flight into Egypt*. Rome, Galleria Doria

in Rome. Only one of these, *The Flight into Egypt* (fig.8) is by Annibale himself, but he certainly planned the whole series and his complete mastery of the new form can be seen by comparing his own work with that of his pupils, who never quite get the relation of figures to landscape right.

The Landscape in *The Flight into Egypt* is not a direct transcription of nature, although it bears a family resemblance to the Roman Campagna. It is built up of a number of motives which were to degenerate into a repertory in the hands of some later imitators—the repoussoir trees which conveniently close the composition at the sides, the flock of sheep trooping down a slope to water, the boatman in a gesture of ingenious contrapposto, the massive building, at once Roman and medieval, the network of diagonals contrived with streams and hillocks. Annibale's figures, unlike those in many of the works of Domenichino, are poetically felt and their mood is quite specific, and he has contrived to make them the emotional pivot of the composition by ingenious play with his diagonals. The ground slopes away to right, but the Holy Family are moving downwards to left: these two diagonals cross at the crucial point where the ass resolves the discord by moving his head round out of the line of his body. The creation of this kind of ideal landscape, which served equally as a setting for small figures from mythological or religious stories, was one of the great inventions of European painting in the seventeenth century, which was to be most fully exploited by the French painters settled in Rome, Nicolas and Gaspard Poussin and Claude.

A nervous melancholy settled on Annibale Carracci about 1605 and he seems to have painted little between that year and his death in 1609, but some of the most

9. GUIDO RENI: *The Crucifixion of S. Peter*. Vatican, Gallery

distinguished pupils of the Carracci Academy in Bologna had followed him to Rome, and Bolognese Classicism was to be the prevailing style for fresco decoration in Rome for the first quarter of the seventeenth century.

Three of these pupils of the Bolognese Academy deserve special attention in the Roman scene: Guido Reni (1575–1642), Francesco Albano (1578–1660) and Domenichino (1581–1641). Guido, the eldest of them, was already a mature artist when he first came to Rome, with Albano, in 1601. He had been grounded in art at Bologna under Denys Calvert, whose late Mannerism he had completely abandoned when he transferred his studies to the Carracci Academy about 1595, but on his first visit to Rome he was still open to other influences than Classicism, and Caravaggio's powerfully dramatic style, with its violent contrasts of light and shade was for the moment fashionable in certain exalted circles of patronage. One of Guido's first major works in Rome, painted in 1604–1605, was the *Crucifixion of S. Peter* (fig.9) now in the Vatican Gallery. This is an ingenious attempt to marry the Bolognese style, with its decorous models, studied composition, and suggestion of landscape setting, to Caravaggio's bold effects of lighting. How much it must have exasperated Caravaggio can be seen by comparing it with his *Flagellation* in S. Domenico Maggiore at Naples (fig.146), where a subject at least as gruesome is treated with an altogether different kind of realism. Guido had his supporters at this time, but, when he returned to Rome in 1607, Caravaggismo was no longer so fashionable and he veered at once in the direction of a full Classicism, which was to be the main element in his later style.

Caravaggio's flight from Rome in 1606, under suspicion of murder, seems to have brought 'Caravaggismo' into some disrepute even in Papal circles, although the Borghese had been among his best patrons—and, in any case, he was incapable of fresco painting. Annibale was a prey to melancholia and Cardinal Borghese turned to Guido, as to the leader of the Bolognese school in Rome, for a variety of important commissions—for frescoes in the Chapel of S. Andrea attached to S. Gregorio on the Celian; for frescoes (1608) in certain minor rooms in the Vatican; and for the Borghese Chapel in Sta Maria Maggiore. But the commission which produced Guido's masterpiece was for the ceiling of the Casino attached to the huge Palace the Borghese were building on the Quirinal, which is now the Palazzo Rospigliosi-Pallavicini. This was the *Aurora* (fig.10) which was painted in 1613/14, and is planned like an easel picture (what was called a *quadro riportato*) on the flat centre of the ceiling in a frame of extremely elegant stuccoes, which blossom out at both ends into sirens set at right angles to the main design and supporting small semi-circular frescoes of wind-blowing cherubs. These comfort the eye when the spectator is standing at either end of the room. The fresco is a conscious, and completely successful attempt, in the wake of Raphael, to achieve the imagined style of classical painting. The figures move in a slow dancing rhythm from left to right, in the

10. GUIDO RENI: *Aurora*. Rome, Casino Rospigliosi

spirit of an ancient relief. The forms and features are of an ideal beauty which avoids both insipidity and the suggestion of the model. The colouring is gay and fresh and the landscape at the right, with a vast expanse of blue sea and distant headlands, is captivatingly lovely. It is the great monument of the moment of calm before the storm of the full Baroque was to break. Ten years later, Guercino's *Aurora* (fig.98) in the Casino Ludovisi marks the abandonment of all those tranquil virtues which Guido cherished. A few months after this crowning achievement of his Roman period, Guido, for reasons which are not wholly clear, returned to Bologna, where, on the death of Ludovico Carracci in 1619, he came to dominate the Bolognese school (see pp. 93 ff.).

Guido's departure left Domenichino (Domenico Zampieri) as the leading figure among the Bolognese Classicists in Rome. His artistic personality was much more positive than that of Albano, who followed Guido to Bologna in 1616 and left in Rome only one major decoration, the Gallery of the Palazzo Verospi, which is somewhat difficult of access. Domenichino seems to have been Annibale's favourite pupil, and he shared his master's devotion to careful preparatory drawings as well as his nervous melancholy. He developed Annibale's final style a little further in the direction of a meditative Classicism, drawing his inspiration from the same models as his master, but he has a sufficiently personal imprint to rank as a great master, and it is not for nothing that his art was revered by Poussin. As a painter of large-scale decorations he outlived his age by a decade, and his work in the Cathedral of Naples in the 1630's is troubled by an awareness of, but no sympathy for, the Baroque.

Domenichino's art may be most easily liked in the many landscapes, forerunners of Claude's, peopled with small figures from sacred or pagan story, which are widely distributed through all the great collections. But his major works are mostly in fresco and are still to be found in the neighbourhood of Rome. The earliest (about 1605) are tenderly poetic landscapes, which now have almost the pale tone of watercolour, with stories from Ovid, which once adorned an outside Loggia in the Palazzo Farnese, but have now been detached and are exhibited in one of the public rooms of the Palace. But his style matured rapidly, at first in competition with Guido in the Chapel of S. Andrea attached to S. Gregorio (1608), and then in the narrative scenes from the *Life of S. Nilus* commissioned by Cardinal Odoardo Farnese for the Badia of Grottaferrata (1608/10). It was about this time that Domenichino lived in some intimacy with Monsignor Giovanni Battista Agucchi, the earliest of those seventeenth-century amateur art-theorists who played a considerable part in determining the official taste of the time, and eventually won the battle for Classicism against the Baroque. Domenichino's admirable portrait of Agucchi is in the City Art Gallery at York (fig.11), and it is surely no accident that his most pondered and memorable works should date from the time when he was most closely in touch with Agucchi and constantly discussing with him the

11. DOMENICHINO: *Portrait of Monsignor Agucchi.*
York, City Art Gallery

theoretical principles of Classicism. These are the altarpiece with *The Last Communion of S. Jerome* (fig.12) of 1614, from S. Girolamo della Carità, now in the Vatican Gallery, and the frescoes in S. Luigi dei Francesi.

The *S. Jerome* was considered for two and a half centuries as one of the great pictures of the world. It is only now that we are beginning to look again at pictures of this period without prejudice, that we can see that this was a perfectly sound judgment. If it were cleaned there could be no doubt. Taking over the superficial details of the pattern (the arched opening and cherubs in the sky) from a too-famous work of twenty years earlier by Agostino Carracci (Bologna, Gallery), Domenichino, by rearranging every gesture, every character, and the relation of the group to the architecture and the landscape, in the interests of solemnity and the human dignity of the story, has produced a dramatic *tableau* of the greatest poignancy. It is the ideal altarpiece of its decade, harmonizing with the severe lines of early Baroque altars, telling its story with admirable directness and clearness when seen from afar, and profoundly concerned with the ideal rendering of specific emotions on the face of each participant.

Hardly less splendid, when they were in their original state, must have been the frescoes in the Chapel of S. Cecilia (1613/14) in the dark and rather ugly Church of

12. DOMENICHINO: *The Last Communion of S. Jerome*. Vatican, Gallery

13. DOMENICHINO: *S.Cecilia distributing Clothes to the Poor*. Rome, S.Luigi dei Francesi

S. Luigi dei Francesi. Of these the *S. Cecilia distributing Clothes to the Poor* (fig.13) is still sufficiently readable to the sympathetic eye. The figure style is a restatement in the tenderer terms of its time of Raphael's *Fire in the Borgo*. It is framed in a moulding like an easel picture and it is all in browns and greys and greens, with no strong colours. Each figure, and each complicated group, has been studied with extraordinary refinement and it is not surprising that later painters, down to the time of Reynolds and Alan Ramsay, should have made drawings from it in pursuit of models for 'grace' and elegance. Echoes of it also appear constantly in the work of Poussin, who worked in Domenichino's studio soon after his arrival in Rome in 1624.

The last wholly successful fresco decoration completed by Domenichino was the adornment of the spandrels of the cupola and of the semi-dome of the apse in Maderno's S. Andrea della Valle—the last church in Rome by a major Baroque architect (until the very end of the century) to be designed so as to allow the painter a major role in its interior effect. Domenichino had hoped for the cupola too, but

14. DOMENICHINO: *S. John Evangelist*. Rome, S. Andrea della Valle

that commission was given to Lanfranco. The apse frescoes were begun in 1623 and perhaps completed in 1627, and the *Four Evangelists* in the spandrels are documented as 1627/28. The decorative intentions of each series are curiously different. The apse frescoes must have been designed while Domenichino still hoped for the dome and when he had no thought of competition with anything which we should now call Baroque: but the spandrels were painted after Lanfranco had completed his triumphant *Assumption* (fig.36). These *Evangelists* (cf. fig.14) are heroic figures of remarkable power, beautifully conforming in scale to the vast size of the church- much more so than Lanfranco's figures above them. They float in a white empyrean (neither sky nor gold, but simply 'space'), filling their triangles and bursting out of them at the same time, and they contrive to combine harmoniously the might of Michelangelo with the grace of Correggio. They are by far the finest spandrel decoration in Rome, and they make Domenichino's own later spandrels (at S. Carlo ai Catinari and at Naples) look fussy and Baciccia's in the Gesu look tousled.

15. DOMENICHINO: *S. John Baptist revealing Christ to SS. Peter and Andrew.*
Rome, S. Andrea della Valle

They show what Domenichino could do, when spurred by rivalry with Lanfranco, in the new style. But one can hardly doubt that the apse frescoes, with their quite different stylistic intentions, represent his preferred taste.

The semidome of the apse is divided into triangular compartments by stucco strips of great elegance, which were designed by Domenichino himself. In these are three stories from the life of S. Andrew, with figures on a very modest scale, which do not compete at all with the scale of the Church. Below these are upright panels of the Virtues, and, set in a most elaborate stucco frame, on the under surface of the entrance arch, is the masterpiece of the series, *The Baptist revealing Christ to SS. Peter and Andrew* (fig. 15). These dramatic figures in a splendid Venetian landscape make an easel picture of the highest quality which happens to have to be seen in the most inconvenient possible position. This sets the tone for what was to be a dilemma for the Classicists throughout the century and reaches its *reductio ad absurdum* in Sacchi's paintings hung invisibly in the dome of S. Giovanni in Fonte. The anti-Baroque painter, according to this line of reasoning, must treat his picture space with all the scrupulous refinement needed to be seen at the level of the eye, and he simply need not worry about the inconvenient position from which it will have to be seen. The opposite pole to this will be seen in Fratel Pozzo's ceiling in S. Ignazio.

2 : CARAVAGGIO

DURING the years 1595 to 1606, when Annibale Carracci was establishing the canons for a style which was to be the most influential in Rome throughout the seventeenth century, the flight from Mannerism was being pursued by other painters on other lines. The most famous in international repute of the old Mannerist gang, Federico Zuccaro (c. 1543–1609), already anticipated the change of taste in his disarmingly simple narrative frescoes of the *Life of S. Hyacinth* (c. 1595) in S. Sabina and in the altarpiece of the same date of the *Adoration of the Kings* in Lucca Cathedral, which goes back in style to Bellini: and conservative Papal and official taste during these years favoured the less radical innovations of Cesari d'Arpino (see p. 5). It was natural that a young painter from Lombardy of great ambition but little experience, arriving in Rome about 1591/92, should have sought to attach himself as an assistant to Arpino.

This young man was Michelangelo Merisi (1573–1610), called from the small town of his birth in Lombardy *il Caravaggio*. He had been apprenticed for four years, from 1584, to a Milanese painter of sufficient competence, Simone Peterzano, and he had trained his eye in the Veneto-Lombard tradition of painting of the sixteenth century, which may be said to have begun with Giorgione and to have been continued by his followers at Brescia and Bergamo, Savoldo, Moretto and Lotto. Giorgione had created the 'fancy picture', in which a single figure or group establishes a poetic mood without being tied down to any strict subject matter; he liked figures in fancy dress; and he seems to have made experiments in the nocturne. A liking for rich fabrics and the play of light and strong shadow upon them had been carried further by Savoldo, who had left important examples of his art at Milan. These are the more obvious precedents which help to account for the general bent of the handful of pictures by the young Caravaggio which survive from the period before about 1597.

So much fancy ink has been spilled about Caravaggio during the last thirty-five years, and he has been credited with roles of such extravagant importance in the history of art (not all of them mutually compatible), that his true quality is very hard to discern and the innocent reader of art-historical literature could be forgiven for supposing that his place in the history of civilization lies somewhere in importance between Aristotle and Lenin. He had artistic gifts of the highest order, but, as his tragic life abundantly shows, he altogether lacked patience. He never learned drawing, in the academic sense of the discipline, and he liked to paint direct from the model—so he made a virtue of this and proclaimed that everyone was a fool who didn't do likewise. As a corollary to this, when he first arrived in Rome, he had no notion how to build up a composition which involved a number of figures: and he never mastered the art of fresco painting, which was the one road to the greatest reputations in Italian painting. Feeling, we may suppose, some inferiority from these weaknesses, he built up a legend about himself as the great revolutionary for whom the art of the past meant nothing, while the life about him, which he painted direct and unadorned, was everything. But this was very far from the truth.

He perhaps started out as a specialist in the painting of still life, and especially of fruit. Studies of single figures followed, but they are clumsier than the fruit which gives them their savour of originality and charm—for Caravaggio's models at this period were either himself or young persons who have an air of being promising but depraved. The Uffizi *Bacchus*, without the saving grace of its still life, would be a very disagreeable picture indeed. But he painted at least one pure still life—the *Basket of Fruit* in the Ambrosiana, Milan (fig.16)—in which his poetic genius is perfectly clear. Although the ground has been repainted, this is *not* a fragment, but one of the first still-life paintings to proclaim, by the nobility of its design and the decorative subtlety of its arrangement, that inanimate nature was as proper a subject for serious painting as the human figure. This was probably painted in 1596 for Cardinal del Monte, Caravaggio's first patron from the great world, whose

16. CARAVAGGIO: *A Basket of Fruit*. Milan, Ambrosiana

influence was to redirect the artist towards the field of religious art. His first commission for the Cardinal, painted a year or two earlier, had been the *Concert* (Metropolitan Museum, New York; fig.17), his first ambitious figure group, which is an attempt to restate the poetic qualities of Giorgione's *Concert champêtre* in

17. CARAVAGGIO: *A Concert*. New York, Metropolitan Museum

terms of low life and with the tavern replacing the rural scene. What the picture is 'about' might be debated for ever, but it seems to have been understood as a statement about the romantic possibilities of the flash underworld, which seems to have won the approval of a substantial group of picture collectors and of a number of young painters of the next generation, especially foreigners. For the Frenchman, le Valentin, and a group of Dutchmen working in Rome in the second decade of the seventeenth century, turned out a steady stream of pictures with raffish themes from a Bohemian Arcadia, which spread the genre throughout Western Europe. But Caravaggio himself abandoned it as soon as he had received, about 1597, his first major Church commission.

At an unknown date during his first years in Rome Caravaggio fell sick, probably of malaria, and entered the Hospital della Consolazione. It may have been here that he first came into contact with the Congregation of the Oratory, which had been founded by S. Philip Neri, and one of whose most energetically pursued activities was the visiting of Hospitals. It is certain that his most important patrons during his second Roman period, which runs to 1606, belonged to Oratorian circles, and Caravaggio's most famous altarpiece, the *Deposition* (fig.18) was painted for the Oratorian Church of S. Maria in Vallicella. But more important is the fact that

18. CARAVAGGIO: *The Deposition*. Vatican, Gallery

his profoundly original religious style, which is humble and realistic, emotionally profound and (to many contemporaries) embarrassingly lacking in class-consciousness, reflects more than that of any other painter the unostentatious piety of the Oratorians. The transformation of a style nourished on the realistic representation of the seedier underworld into an instrument for devotional art presented Caravaggio with considerable difficulties—and so did the composition of elaborate groups with an emotional content to a painter who had limited himself to the single figure or the arrangement of figures without narrative cohesion. By the time he was forced to fly from Rome in 1606 as the result of an impulsive homicide, he had mastered both these problems.

The earliest of his religious paintings, which probably slightly antedates the commission in 1597 for the paintings in S. Luigi dei Francesi, is the *Rest on the Flight into Egypt* in the Doria Gallery in Rome (fig.19). It is not an accident that this picture should so strangely remind us of the work of the young English 'Pre-Raphaelites' in the nineteenth century, for the spirit in which it was conceived is the same as theirs. The figures are studied from humble models, friends or neighbours, and have a certain portrait-like quality: the setting of the group in a poetic landscape, studied in a spirit of still life in the foreground and with an impression

19. CARAVAGGIO: *The Rest on the Flight into Egypt*. Rome, Galleria Doria

Detail from fig. 19

of shadowed mystery in the lovely background to right, is a return to an earlier Venetian tradition, perhaps to Lotto: the deliberately naïve motive of S. Joseph holding up the music from which the angel plays, gives a suggestion that everything must be studied from the life and not vamped out of one's head—and all these elements in the picture would have been very sympathetic to Holman Hunt. But Caravaggio must soon have become aware of the clumsy way in which the axis of the angel's body cuts the picture in half, and he probably found that the effort of surrounding his realistic figures with an equally realistic representation of the outside world gave him more trouble than it was worth from the point of view of the emotional content of the picture. He certainly never repeated the experiment and turned to dark backgrounds and a system of irrational lighting, which has a misleading air of realism but is exploited with the greatest poetic licence.

It was through Cardinal del Monte that Caravaggio received the commission to complete the painting of the Contarelli Chapel in S. Luigi dei Francesi, which had been left with only the ceiling painted by Cesari d'Arpino. The commission was given in 1597 and required three paintings: an altarpiece with *S. Matthew and the*

20. CARAVAGGIO: *The Calling of S.Matthew*. Rome, S.Luigi dei Francesi

Angel, and two large canvases on the side walls representing *The Calling* (fig.20) and *The Martyrdom of S. Matthew*. The first version of the altarpiece (which was later in the Berlin Gallery and one of the pictures which were destroyed in 1945) was rejected by the Church as being altogether too indecorous for an altarpiece, and was later replaced by a second picture in which the Saint is much less plebeian and the angelic inspiration is given in a more aloof manner. The two large side canvases also gave a lot of trouble and were not completed until about 1601. X-rays have revealed that the *Martyrdom* was wholly reworked and it is perfectly plain that Caravaggio learned how to compose 'histories' on these long-suffering canvases, and learned with considerable difficulty, though his task was made fairly easy in *The Calling of S. Matthew* from the fact that it is one of the few New Testament subjects which lends itself to low-life *genre*, and the frustrated young person who is leaning on the future Apostle's side is an admirable piece of comedy and wholly in line with Caravaggio's earlier paintings. This picture may have had some influence on le Valentin, but these pictures must always have been nearly as invisible as they are today, and it is better to judge Caravaggio's earlier religious style from the two side

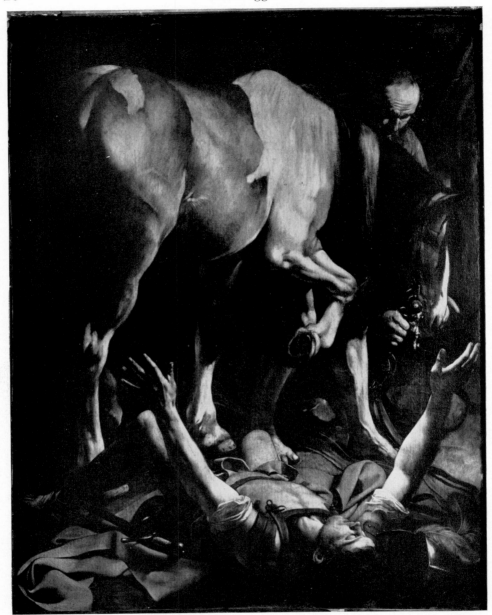

21. CARAVAGGIO: *The Conversion of S.Paul*. Rome, S.Maria del Popolo

pictures painted in 1601 for the Cerasi Chapel in Sta Maria del Popolo, where he had to compete with an altarpiece by Annibale Carracci.

The more striking of these is *The Conversion of S. Paul* (fig.21). As Leo Steinberg has pointed out, it was never meant to be seen head on, as it appears in a photograph. It was on the right-hand wall of a narrow chapel, and intended to be seen

22. CARAVAGGIO: *The Death of the Virgin*. Paris, Louvre

23. CARAVAGGIO: *The Beheading of S. John Baptist*. Valletta, Cathedral

obliquely (as was its opposite companion, *The Crucifixion of S. Peter*). The arrangement of these two pictures, conceived as receiving their light from a painted glory in the ceiling of the chapel, is deliberately illusionistic. Caravaggio has done everything possible to bring home to the spectator the vivid immediacy of the scene, as if he were witnessing the incident himself, rather than as if he were looking at a picture of it. The intention is not different from that recommended by the Jesuit *Exercises*, and the picture, viewed in this light, has the hallucinatory quality of a vision beheld by the spectator himself. It is a new kind of religious painting, and it is hardly surprising that it was neither understood nor considered acceptable by conservative religious opinion. Caravaggio employed the same principles in the two other most memorable altarpieces which he painted for Roman churches between 1601 and his flight from Rome in 1606—the *Deposition* (Vatican Gallery; fig.18), painted 1602/4 for the Oratorian Church of S. Maria in Vallicella, and *The Death of the Virgin* (Paris, Louvre; fig.22) painted 1605/6 for S. Maria della Scala, but rejected because the Carmelites considered it altogether too indecorous. We are so accustomed today to seeing classical tragedy 'in modern dress' that the full impact of astonishment which these pictures set up passes us by. *The Death of the Virgin* was painted for a church in the poorer parts of the Trastevere, and malicious gossip related that the figure of the Virgin had been painted from a drowned strumpet who had been fished out of the river. Such tales were a tribute to Caravaggio's humane naturalism and profound religious feeling, which was not alien to the Oratorians' idea of Christian charity, but was looked on with ill-favour by more conservative circles in the age of the Counter-Reformation. What strikes us most today is the immense dignity and weight of human compassion which these pictures exhale.

Caravaggio fled from Rome, under the imputation of murder, in May 1606. By the end of the year he was in Naples, where he painted two altarpieces, which are still *in situ*, within a few months, and effected a revolution in the local school of painting (see pp. 170 ff.). For a year, 1607/8, he was in Malta, painting with an energy and expedition unknown to his Roman years, until his hot temper again led to disaster, but it was during this feverish period that he painted his most astonishing masterpiece, *The Beheading of S. John Baptist* in the Cathedral of Valletta (fig.23). This enormous picture measures about 12 by 17 feet. The action seems to take place on a stage and the cast has been brilliantly chosen from common nature. The main figures form a group of the most classic severity, but the gesture of each is of an inspired naturalness. The movement of Salome might seem to have been forced by the exigences of the design, if it were not explained by her overmastering reluctance not to witness the deed of horror. And the illusion of the space, which not only envelopes the actors but the spectator as well—as has become apparent now that the picture has been cleaned—is almost overpowering. This inducement to the spectator to participate in the action of the picture is a characteristic of the Roman

24. CARAVAGGIO: *The Nativity*. Messina, Museum

full Baroque style, although the machinery employed by later Baroque painters was very far removed from Caravaggio's naturalism.

Escaping from prison in Malta, Caravaggio fled to Sicily, where he spent less than a year (1608/9) evading the Grand Master's agents and leaving behind altarpieces at Messina, Syracuse and Palermo. The *Martyrdom of S. Lucy* (Syracuse, S. Lucia) and the *Raising of Lazarus* (Messina, Museo) are dramatic inventions in the vein of the picture at Valletta, but the *Nativity* (Messina, Museo; fig.24) has an astonishing vein of tenderness..Battered though it is, almost without colour, it is rivalled—but not surpassed—in depth of feeling only by certain inventions of Rembrandt: and in Rembrandt there is more artifice to be discerned than there is in this picture by Caravaggio. In a hectic career of less than twenty years, marked to the outside view by increasing signs of arrogance and violence, Caravaggio had changed from a smart painter of low.life into one of the most moving religious painters of modern times. We know nothing of the inner compulsions which went on inside him, but the continuing patronage of some of the more enlightened church dignitaries shows that there was something about his character more than the police record or the gossip of art-historians reveals. But his earliest patron, Cardinal del Monte, called him a 'cervello stravagantissimo', which means something like 'a very odd genius indeed'. His fame remained high throughout the whole seventeenth century, but the question of his influence is much more difficult to assess.

3 : THE CARAVAGGESCHI

ANNIBALE Carracci was a natural teacher and his pupils understood his teaching and carried on his tradition. Both his method and his temperament made Caravaggio alike incapable of taking a pupil or of imparting to others the profound and sensitive feeling which inspired his religious pictures. But these pictures were memorable and exciting for other qualities as well and a whole generation of young painters, native and foreign, was captivated by them and tried to imitate their dramatic lighting: and the low-life *genre* of Caravaggio's earlier pictures also produced a crop of imitators. It is customary to call these the 'Caravaggeschi' and to refer to that style of painting in which strongly lit figures are seen against a dark ground as 'Caravaggismo'. The term Caravaggeschi is legitimate as applied to the painters about to be discussed and to a number of Flemish and French painters who studied in Rome in the second decade of the seventeenth century: but it seems likely that a liking for strongly lit figures against a dark interior was a mark of the times and developed in, for instance, the young Velasquez and the young Guercino, quite independently of any direct or mediate influence from Caravaggio, and it is begging a number of questions to use the term 'Caravaggismo' to mean anything more than

25. ELSHEIMER: *The Flight into Egypt*. Paris, Louvre

'a *tenebroso* style of which Caravaggio was one of the principal exponents'. There was also another painter in Rome who was important for creating the particular artistic climate, which is the background for the work of the Caravaggeschi. This was the German landscape painter Adam Elsheimer (1578–1610).

Elsheimer, who spent the last ten years of his life in Rome, was the first great master of the romantic Landscape, which was to play such a large role in European seventeenth-century painting. His best work is on a small, sometimes on a minute scale, and upon copper. He is haunted alike by memories of northern woodlands and streams and by the larger sweep of the Roman Campagna: he likes especially effects of twilight: and he enlarges the poetic content of his scenes by little figures taken from classical or bible story (fig.25). Much of the later work of Claude is Elsheimer writ large, in the grand manner. Elsheimer's Landscapes are intimate and tender in contrast with the generalized public prospects of the Carracci land-scape tradition. Rubens, who was his friend, learned much from his art and also from that of Caravaggio. The art of the two was complementary, and the influence of both can be discerned in the work of the two most interesting of the Caravaggeschi, Orazio Gentileschi (1563–1639) and Carlo Saraceni (1579–1620), the only two painters of the group who can have come into direct contact with Caravaggio.

Gentileschi, who was born in Pisa, worked in Rome (perhaps with some inter-ruptions) from 1576 to 1621. Before 1603 he had even been on sufficiently friendly terms with Caravaggio to lend him a Capuchin's cowl and a pair of wings. But it was

26. ORAZIO GENTILESCHI: *The Rest on the Flight into Egypt*. Paris, Louvre

Caravaggio's earlier work (such as the *Rest on the Flight* (fig.19) or the *Magdalen* in the Doria Gallery) which chiefly influenced him, with their emphasis on the play of light on smooth fabrics. He moved away from Caravaggio in a Tuscan liking for prettiness, and it may be doubted if he had formed a positive style of his own before about 1615. He had painted a handful of distinguished altarpieces in the Marche (the best is the *Marriage of S. Catherine* in the Urbino Gallery), before he left for Genoa in 1621. From there he moved to Turin and to Paris (1623/24–1626), and he settled in London in 1626 for the rest of his life as painter to Charles I. He is important as the transmitter of a watered Caravaggesque style to several European Courts, but he grew lazy in later years and spent much of his time repeating, with variations, a handful of designs, of which the most agreeable is the *Rest on the Flight* (Paris, Louvre; fig.26), with its odd combination of naturalism, intimacy and elegance. It is instructive to compare it with Caravaggio's painting of the same subject (fig.19). Saraceni, who was a Venetian, came to Rome *c.* 1598, and fell early under Elsheimer's influence, although he always had aspirations to figure painting. The charming *Rest on the Flight* (Frascati, Camaldoli; fig.27) is dated 1606 and combines Elsheimer's poetic landscape with Caravaggio's lighting and intimate study of the unidealized model. His later development is away from the small scale of Elsheimer towards the monumental. His concern with fabrics is similar to Gentileschi's, but he had a much more delicate feeling for colour and tone. The *Madonna and Child with S. Anne* (Rome, Galleria Nazionale; fig.28), with its gay and enchanting colour

27. SARACENI: *The Rest on the Flight into Egypt*. Frascati, Calmadolese Hermitage

28. SARACENI: *Madonna with S.Anne.*
Rome, Galleria Nazionale

29. BORGIANNI: *The Holy Family.*
Rome, Galleria Nazionale

(cherry, deep blue, lilac and gamboge), shows how a picture can owe as it were the possibility of its being painted to the innovations of Caravaggio, while being as alien to his style as possible within the new conventions of naturalism and strongly contrasted lighting. It is intimate and domestic, in the Venetian tradition: the dark ground is without mystery and makes no positive contribution to the content of the picture, which was an altarpiece for a very small church under aristocratic patronage. In his larger altarpieces—for the Cathedrals of Gaeta and Palestrina—Saraceni was a good deal less successful, but his *Miracle of S. Benno* of 1618 (Rome, S. Maria dell' Anima) is a brilliantly cast naturalistic scene with the same intimate quality.

It is interesting to compare with the Saraceni another *Holy Family* (fig.29) also in the Galleria Nazionale at Rome and of exactly the same date (about 1610/15). This is by Orazio Borgianni (1578?–1616), a Roman painter who went to Spain in the later 1590's, with no Caravaggesque background, and returned to Rome in time to have quarrelled personally with Caravaggio before the latter fled in 1606. Borgianni, in his few surviving works, always attempts a Grand Style. The still life of the cradle (which had been prominent in Saraceni's picture, but is well integrated into its domestic content) is so overwhelmingly impressive in the Borgianni that it steals the picture and is an intrusive element of naturalism in an otherwise classical design. Apart from this Borgianni's style seems to have developed independently of Caravaggio, and his *S. Carlo Borromeo* of 1611/12 (Rome, S. Carlino; fig.30)—one of the first images to be painted after the Saint's canonization—ranks as one of the most impressive and deeply felt religious pictures of the time.

30. BORGIANNI: *S.Charles Borromeo*. Rome, S.Carlino

31. MANFREDI: *A Concert*. Florence, Uffizi

32. VALENTIN: *The Card Players*. Dresden, Gallery

In the second decade of the seventeenth century there seems to have been a struggle for favour between the *tenebroso* style, which looked to Caravaggio as its champion, and those painters who were the heirs of Bolognese Classicism. By about 1623 the latter had won, and the young Guercino, who had painted a handful of masterpieces in Rome under the Pontificate of Gregory XV (1621/23: see pp. 108 ff.), returned to the North to chasten his style according to the new canons of taste.

But this change was confined to religious painting, and the type of low-life *genre* which Caravaggio had introduced in his earliest works was to have a longer success. It was taken up, about 1610, by Bartolommeo Manfredi (*c.* 1582–1620), whose *Concert* (fig.31) in the Uffizi is one of his best attested pictures, and pictures of this subject, card-sharpers and single fancy figures of the same kind, were multiplied by a group of painters from Utrecht, Ter Brugghen, van Baburen and Honthorst, and given international currency. The style was taken to France by Tournier and others, and in Rome it was carried on by another Frenchman, Valentin (1591-1632) who never worked outside Italy and whose identifiable *oeuvre* probably dates from after 1620. He was much the most accomplished of the group and was even commissioned to do an altarpiece in S. Peter's in 1629 by the Barberini *régime*, though it met with little favour. The *Card-sharpers* at Dresden (fig.32) is one of his most carefully planned pictures, both in design and psychology, and the patronage by the great Roman collectors for this kind of picture led on to the triumph of a later type of low-life painting, the *Bambocciate*.

4 : LANFRANCO

THE creators of the two chief masterpieces of High Baroque fresco painting were Giovanni Lanfranco (1582–1647) and Pietro da Cortona. Lanfranco was the pioneer and the link between the Carracci tradition and the style which was to prevail in the age of Urban VIII (Barberini), whose tenure of the Papacy lasted from 1623 to 1644. Something is said elsewhere (pp. 105 ff.) about his early training at Parma, but he is an artist of sufficient stature to deserve considering by himself. For already in a very early picture of about 1605, *The Magdalen transported to Heaven* (Naples, Gallery; fig.33), painted for one of the smaller rooms in the Palazzo Farnese in Rome, he showed his originality in a captivatingly poetical picture. The evening landscape, in blue and silver, with a lake set among the hills of the Roman Campagna, is the first entirely satisfactory image of a countryside, which—largely through the splendid impositions of Claude Lorraine later in the century—was to haunt the imagination of Europe as the ideal setting for ancient story.

33. LANFRANCO: *S.Mary Magdalen being transported to Heaven.* Naples, Gallery

In the year or two he spent at Parma before his second return to Rome in 1612, the renewed influence of Correggio and the powerful and original lighting effects of Schedoni, gave his style that extra fillip, that ability to escape from the staid

34. LANFRANCO: *The Ecstasy of S.Margaret of Cortona*. Florence, Palazzo Pitti

Classicism of the Carracci style, towards the emotionalism which was to be demanded by the Baroque age. This can be seen at its best in *The Ecstasy of S. Margaret of Cortona* (Florence, Pitti; fig.34), a picture of about 1620, which looks backwards to Correggio's *Martyrdom of SS. Placidus and Flavia* and forwards to Bernini's *S. Theresa*, which is the epitome of High Baroque style. The new resources of emotionalism—achieved both by expression and by the grid-pattern of lighting—can be gauged by comparing this picture with Domenichino's *Last Communion of*

35. LANFRANCO: *The Ascension*. Rome, S.Giovanni dei Fiorentini

S. Jerome of 1614 (fig.12), and it is significant that Lanfranco and Domenichino were to be rivals (and bitter antagonists) both at S. Andrea della Valle and in the Chapel of S. Gennaro in Naples Cathedral.

One suspects that Lanfranco returned from Parma determined to try out the lessons of Correggio in the matter of painting domes. His first experiment was on a small scale, the *Ascension* (fig.35) on the ceiling of the Sacchetti Chapel in S. Giovanni dei Fiorentini, painted *c*. 1621/24. This is a sufficiently startling work and it would be interesting to know if it had any influence in securing for Lanfranco the commission to paint the dome of S. Andrea della Valle, which Domenichino, who had painted the apse frescoes (cf. fig.15) confidently expected for himself. The importance of this dome, which represents the *Assumption of the Virgin* (fig.36)— the subject which Correggio had painted a hundred years before in the dome of the Cathedral of Parma—was already recognized in the seventeenth century by Bellori, who considers it as the first great work of a new style and did not think it had been surpassed by later examples. That new style is what we call today the High Baroque, and what most impressed was its quality of unity in diversity. There are an immense number of figures, which can be clearly differentiated by a close scrutiny, but the overwhelming effect is of a single harmony. Bellori talks of a full choir and an orchestra and the analogy is a valuable one to describe the effect produced.

The means by which Lanfranco produces his effects are novel and ingenious. The source of light is in the figure of Christ in a dazzling glory at the top of the

36. LANFRANCO: *The Assumption of the Virgin.* Rome, S.Andrea della Valle

lantern. It produces something of the effect of a powerful electric light bulb, which diffuses its radiance over a huge area by means of a shade: but the shade is a thick wreath of foliage supported by cherubs—an adaptation of another of Correggio's decorative inventions. The diffused flickering of light over the whole dome has something of a hypnotic effect—which was soon to become one of the aims of Baroque architecture. And yet we must remember that none of the great Roman Baroque churches built in the next fifty years allowed any room for painting to achieve these effects. For, although we can see them very well when we study a good photograph, a visit to S. Andrea itself raises some doubts in the mind about how far the illusion of equating the dome with the Heavens was really intended by Lanfranco. For the lower story of the cupola, with its tall windows and white and gold pilasters,

37. LANFRANCO: *The Crucifixion*. Naples, S.Martino

makes nonsense of the illusion—and Domenichino's pendentives, with their mighty figures against a white empyrean, clash with Lanfranco's higher heaven, which has a yellowish glory round the central band of foliage and a sort of bluish glow over the rest. None the less, this dome, which was completed between 1625 and 1627, marks the death-blow to Bolognese Classicism in Rome, and, for the next five years (up to 1631), Lanfranco was one of the team of artists employed in S. Peter's.

It is perhaps to the fact that all the great creative minds of the new generation of artists were employed at the same time at S. Peter's between about 1625 and 1631 that the Baroque style in Rome owes a certain unity which one would not expect from the diversity of individual temperament and theory found in its major figures. The presiding genius and most fertile artistic mind of the age was Bernini, who succeeded Maderno as the architect to S. Peter's in 1629 and was the principal artistic counsellor to the Papacy for the next fifty years. Working also at S. Peter's, in addition to Lanfranco, were Pietro da Cortona, who was to become the greatest master of Baroque decoration, and Andrea Sacchi, his chief rival on the classical side. Nor should the presence in this team be forgotten of Nicolas Poussin and the Caravaggesque Valentin, each of whom painted an altarpiece for S. Peter's at this time.

The grandest of Lanfranco's frescoes in S. Peter's of *Christ walking on the water*, is now so battered and displaced (into the Loggia della Benedizione, which is difficult of access) that it is hard to judge, but the fact that Lanfranco was not one of the painters chosen to decorate the Palazzo Barberini (whose decoration was begun in 1629), suggests that he pleased his patrons less than Pietro da Cortona and Sacchi.

At any rate Lanfranco left Rome for Naples in 1634, where he remained for the next twelve years and painted a great number of frescoes, which did more than anything else to convert the local school from Caravaggesque *tenebroso* canvases to frescoes of a light and airy tone. In the dome of the Chapel of S. Gennaro in the Cathedral (again in rivalry with Domenichino) he painted another glory in the same vein (though less successfully) as that in S. Andrea della Valle, but the one of his Neapolitan frescoes which today tells most effectively is the *Crucifixion* (fig.37) in the choir of the Certosa di S. Martino, whose powerful influence can be seen in Caracciolo's and Stanzione's frescoes in the side chapels of the same church. A year or so before he died in 1647 Lanfranco returned to Rome, where he just had time to complete the fresco in the apse of S. Carlo ai Catinari of *S. Charles Borromeo received into Glory*, which is one of the neglected masterpieces of Baroque illusionism.

5. PIETRO DA CORTONA

ALTHOUGH the credit must go to Lanfranco for having created the first great High Baroque decoration, there can be no doubt that the central personality in the field of painting for this period was Pietro Berrettini (1596–1669), known from the place of his birth as Pietro da Cortona. As an universal artistic genius he ranks only just below Bernini, and as an architect of great individuality he rivals him. The names of his first teachers in painting both before and after he arrived in Rome (about 1613) are known, but they cannot be seen to have made any contribution to his personal style, which he seems to have evolved for himself by devoted study of Raphael and the Antique and the Farnese ceiling. His first patrons, from about 1620, were the Sacchetti, who introduced him to Cardinal Francesco Barberini and his learned secretary, Cassiano dal Pozzo—an *Eminence rose*, whose enlightened patronage assisted a number of the most cultivated artists of the time, Pietro, Poussin, and Pietro Testa. Although the frescoes Pietro executed for the Sacchetti have perished, most of the easel pictures he painted for them during the 1620's have survived in the Capitoline Gallery in Rome, and Pietro's development during this decade can be limpidly seen by comparing the earliest, *The Sacrifice of Polyxena* (fig.38), of the early 1620's, with *The Rape of the Sabines* (fig.39) of about 1629. The basic design is very similar in each. Three groups of figures, dramatically

38. PIETRO DA CORTONA: *The Sacrifice of Polyxena*. Rome, Capitoline Gallery

39. PIETRO DA CORTONA: *The Rape of the Sabines*. Rome, Capitoline Gallery

related to one another, are set in a nicely contrasted arrangement: but whereas, in the earlier picture, the arrangement is more or less frieze-like, set before a dark ground in a way that could be called vaguely 'Caravaggesque', in *The Rape of the Sabines* the figure composition is arranged in depth also and is reinforced by landscape and architecture, while the key of colour has become gay and bright. Pietro's standard facial types, which derive from Greco-Roman sculpture, already appear in the *Polyxena*, and the canon as established in the *Rape of the Sabines* was to achieve international currency and to be carried on by Luca Giordano right into the eighteenth century.

It is noteworthy that the most striking groups in the *Sabines* show more than a casual resemblance to the sculptural groups which Bernini was producing in the early 1620's, and the drapery convention, which is substantially different in the later of the two pictures, conforms with the typical Baroque drapery style which was established by Bernini in his *S. Bibiana* of 1624/26. In fact Pietro first came into contact with Bernini during the period 1624/26 when he painted the frescoes (now sadly battered) along the upper part of the north nave arcade in S. Bibiana, which was Bernini's first architectural commission: and, during the later 1620's, Pietro was working with both Bernini and Lanfranco in S. Peter's. It was from these fruitful contacts, and by the power of his own genius that Pietro da Cortona became qualified to take the leading part in the team of Barberini painters, who were active in the 1630's for the important new buildings being erected for the Pope and his family. Apart from the work going on in S. Peter's, these new buildings were the Capuchin Church (S. Maria della Concezione) which was decorated from 1631 to 1638 at the expense of the Pope's brother, Cardinal Antonio Barberini senior, and the new Palazzo Barberini, on which work was begun in 1629. Cardinal Antonio's patronage was conservative. He commissioned an altarpiece each from Guido and Domenichino and two from Lanfranco, but he also commissioned one each from the three painters of the younger generation, who were to form the team for frescoing the Palazzo Barberini, Pietro da Cortona, Andrea Sacchi and Andrea Camassei (1602–1648/49). Camassei proved a disappointment, but to the other two were allotted the decoration of the two largest rooms in the Palazzo Barberini, and between them, although in opposing camps, they were the dominant figures in Roman painting for the next thirty years. Sacchi was an introverted and shy personality, the repository of the classical tradition and a very slow and deliberate worker of great intellectual distinction: Pietro was an extrovert and capable of undertaking vast tasks with splendid exuberance. Pietro's position as the leading painter of the new age was recognized by his being elected President of the Academy of S. Luke for the four years in succession 1634 to 1638.

After some trial work in a small room and in the Chapel (both of which are now part of the Galleria Nazionale), Pietro was given the commission for the ceiling of the Great Saloon of the Palazzo Barberini, which is the most breathtaking achieve-ment of Roman Baroque painting (fig.40). Begun in 1633, it was not completed until 1639, after an interruption of about a year (1637) when Pietro visited Florence and Venice, and it may well be that the impact of Veronese's ceilings, seen in Venice, on the final result was considerable. But the pictorial ancestry of this profoundly original ceiling is numerous and varied. It is entirely executed in fresco, and not (as Pietro's later ceilings in the Palazzo Pitti in Florence were to be) in a mixture of stucco and fresco, although the architectural frame-work, which separates the several scenes, and relates the ceiling to the walls, is made to appear as if of stucco. Although this owes something to the Bolognese *quadratura* painters (see p. 102), its use and intention are quite novel. The immensely intricate corner structures (fig.41), with struggling, rather than placid, figures, enable one scene to melt into its neighbour: and the way the figures float about in front of the central structure give it something of the air of the open top of a greenhouse; and the remarkable thing is that, at whatever point in the room one stands, there is always a part of the ceiling which is best seen from that particular spot. It achieves its complicated decorative intentions with such complete success, that it can hardly be imitated—and in fact it remained unique.

The programme for the fresco decoration of the Palace was devised by Francesco Bracciolini, the official poet of the Barberini circle, but the text of it has not survived, although there is a fairly full account of it in Tetius's *Aedes Barberinae*, from which it is clear that each figure had a precise significance. It is an Allegory of Divine Providence (just as Sacchi's fresco is an Allegory of Divine Wisdom) achieving her ends through the agency of the Barberini Pope, whose personality and mission are artfully indicated by the Papal insignia surmounting a wreath held by Faith, Hope and Charity, in the middle of which are three enormous Barberini bees. The scenes around the edge, whose detail owes a good deal to Virgil, are illustrations, taken from classical mythology, of the virtuous aims of Urban's policy. Each is an elaborate and carefully planned allegory—for instance (fig.42) Religion and Faith are seen overcoming Earthly Love in the shape of Venus, who is surrounded by two groups in which a good Cupid overcomes a bad one. Pietro has transformed the literary programme into visual and decorative terms with remarkable mastery. The effect at which he aims is a knock-out blow and has nothing to do with elegance.

Elegance, however, was his decorative aim in the frescoes which he executed in the Pitti Palace in Florence from 1640 to 1647 (see pp. 161 ff.). Here he employed real stucco and was able to combine his gifts as both architect and painter, but it is curious that, in his own church buildings (and notably in SS. Luca e Martina) he allowed no place for fresco painting. His style does not materially change after the Barberini ceiling, although, in his later Roman years (after 1647) he painted many distinguished altarpieces and easel pictures. The best of his later works are the

40. PIETRO DA CORTONA: Ceiling of the Great Saloon in the Palazzo Barberini, Rome

41–42. PIETRO DA CORTONA: Details of the ceiling of the Palazzo Barberini

43. PIETRO DA CORTONA: *The Battle of Issus*. Rome, Capitoline Gallery

frescoes on the dome, apse and nave ceiling of S. Maria in Vallicella, on which he was fitfully engaged from 1647 till 1665: and the painting of the ceiling of the Galleria in the Palazzo Pamphily (1651 to 1654), which was the family palace of Urban's successor, Innocent X.

Of his easel pictures the Battlepiece in the Capitoline Gallery, of *Alexander's defeat of Darius* (fig.43), deserves special mention. Painted probably during the time he was at work on the Barberini ceiling, about 1635, it is the parent picture of a whole new genre, which was later taken up by Salvator Rosa and Jacques Courtois

44. PIETRO DA CORTONA: Detail of the ceiling in the Palazzo Pamphily, Rome

45. PIETRO DA CORTONA: *The Vision of S.Filippo Neri*. Rome, Chiesa Nuova

46. ROMANELLI: *Countess Matilda receiving Pope Gregory VII at Canossa.*
Vatican Palace

('il Borgognone') and was to have a numerous following in France and the Nether-lands. Although it goes back to Raphael's fresco in the Sala di Costantino in the Vatican, Pietro's is the first major easel picture in the new genre which particularly lent itself to Baroque violence and ordered confusion.

The Galleria of the Palazzo Pamphily was a long narrow room, designed by Borromini, and very different from Bernini's huge square room in the Palazzo Barberini. It is also not very high and a unitary treatment for the fresco painting was impossible. Pietro painted a variety of scenes from the Aeneid (Aeneas was the fabled ancestor of the Pamphily family) and arranged them so that different scenes fall into view as one proceeds down the Gallery. Here too he did not use real stuccoes but he reverts to *stucchi finti* of remarkable elegance (fig.44), which give evidence of his experience with the real stuccoes in the Palazzo Pitti.

Pietro's last major work of fresco decoration was the ceiling of the nave of

S. Maria in Vallicella (fig.45), on which, in 1664/65, he painted the *Vision of S. Filippo Neri while the Church was under construction* within a sharply defined frame, semicircular at either end and surrounded by gold and white stuccoes which were probably designed by himself. There is no attempt at illusion here, although the perspective is not that of an easel picture. The *decorative* intention seems to have been to produce a painting of broad sweep and lively movement, which will do something to give a Baroque air to a church interior designed on Pre-Baroque lines. It is ingenious and successful, but remains something of an oddity, and the fixed shape of the frame indicates a turning away from the High Baroque and a certain resistance to the ideals of Bernini.

Cortona's style was carried on with remarkable purity by Ciro Ferri (1634–1689), who watered it a little, but made no serious additions of his own, and his only early pupil of any marked originality was Giovanni Francesco Romanelli (1610?–1662). Romanelli's style derives from Pietro's earliest works with their Berninesque draperies, and his temperament was placid and with a natural leaning towards the Raphaelesque. He is always without excited movement and is something of a transitional figure between Cortona and Sacchi. Incomparably his most attractive works are the frescoes in the rather inaccessible Sala della Contessa Matilda in the Vatican, which were painted between 1637 and 1642. The scene of *Countess Matilda receiving Gregory VII at Canossa* (fig.46) is enchantingly gracious and the Countess, in honey-yellow, bright blue and violet, is typical of Romanelli's charm and style at its best. It was this style which he conveyed to Paris (following the Barberini into exile) on two visits in 1646/47 and 1655/57, where he did a certain amount of work in the Louvre and elsewhere and profoundly influenced Le Sueur.

6 : SACCHI AND THE CLASSICAL REACTION

IT IS possible to regard the High Baroque as an intrusion into the main tradition of Roman painting, and Pietro da Cortona and Bernini were both 'outsiders'. More conservative opinion still looked to the Antique and Raphael as the founders of true art and believed that the line of succession had followed by way of Annibale Carracci and Domenichino. In the event this classical tradition was to prevail, but it undoubtedly took second place during the middle decades of the century. Just as Algardi represents the classical opposition to Bernini in sculpture, Andrea Sacchi (1599–1661) was the classical opponent to Pietro da Cortona in painting. He had been trained under Albano and emerged in the 1620's as the second leading figure in the Barberini *équipe* of painters. His trouble was that he was extremely deliberate and selfcritical, a master of the carefully considered easel picture or altarpiece, but temperamentally unfitted for vast undertakings, especially in fresco.

47. SACCHI: *The Miracle of S.Gregory*. Rome, S.Peter's

In the work undertaken for Urban VIII in S. Peter's he perhaps at first acquitted himself with greater distinction than either Lanfranco or Pietro da Cortona. The *Miracle of S. Gregory* (fig.47) in the Chapter House of the Canonica of S. Peter's, painted 1625/27, is one of the great masterpieces among the devotional altarpieces of the age, richer in colour and more interesting in paint surface than Pietro's work at this date, and with that careful attention to the psychology of each participant in the scene, which was beyond Pietro's interests and goes back to Raphael's cartoons. The miracle portrayed is similar in character to that shown in Raphael's *Mass of Bolsena*, but Sacchi has transposed Raphael into a fully Baroque design and it is significant that he also employs a very limited number of figures, all of them

48. SACCHI: *The Divine Wisdom*. Rome, Palazzo Barberini

strictly relevant to the emotional content of the story. The other four small altar-pieces of 1633/34 which Sacchi painted for the same place share, though in a less superlative degree, the same virtues.

Unfortunately this work led the Barberini to commission Sacchi to paint the ceiling fresco of the next largest room in the Palazzo Barberini to that painted by Pietro da Cortona. This is the ceiling (now in the Galleria Nazionale) with *The Divine Wisdom* (fig.48), which caused the painter endless trouble and was completed between 1629 and 1633. In spite of admirable drawing and the great intellectual effort displayed this fresco, as decoration, is a disaster—and one can hardly doubt that Sacchi knew this and that it increased his morbid feeling of insufficiency to achieve his aims. This too has no more figures than are strictly necessary to the fable and the comparison, on this score, is very marked with Pietro's fresco in the

49. SACCHI: *The Vision of S.Romuald.*
Vatican, Gallery

Galleria. In fact this question of the number of figures and the method of story-telling was to become a major point of academic controversy in the 1630's. Missirini, the historian of the Academy of S. Luke, gives a summary of certain disputes which occurred at the Academy between the partisans of Sacchi and Pietro da Cortona. Sacchi maintained that 'a picture should be likened to a Tragedy, which was the better when the greatest effect was achieved by the smallest number of players'—which was as much as to set up *The Divine Wisdom* against Pietro's *Allegory of Divine Providence*. The parties seem to have been more or less evenly divided, but the Cortoneschi are rather given away by Missirini's comment that these painters 'did not expect the spectator to examine minutely the details of their pictures: in fact, to prevent them from doing that, they set before them a splendid, harmonious and lively general effect, which would provoke marvel and surprise'. Sacchi was all on the side of brain work, and the greatest painter in Rome at this

50. SACCHI: *The Baptism of Christ*. Rome, S.Giovanni in Fonte

time, Nicolas Poussin, supported him. But Poussin latterly worked only for private clients, mainly Frenchmen like himself, and one can hardly include him in a history of Roman painting.

Sacchi's measured grandeur appears in the few major works of his mature years. The finest is the *Vision of S. Romuald* (*c.* 1631/2; fig.49) in the Vatican Gallery, in which the Saint is recounting his vision to a number of Camaldolese monks. There is no movement and the drama is entirely psychological. The spectator must examine minutely the expression on each face, and the effect aimed at is the reverse of 'surprise'. Sacchi always aims at an *andante maestoso* and, in what is perhaps his greatest and most ambitious series of pictures, the *Stories from the Life of S. John* in the lantern of the Lateran Baptistery, he was barely concerned whether the pictures were visible at all. All eight canvases are extremely carefully studied—the *Baptism* (fig.50) is perhaps the most beautiful—and contain no unnecessary figures: there are exquisite arrangements of balancing movements and all the pictures deserve to be minutely examined—yet it can never have been possible to study them closely at all once they were set up in their intended positions.

51. SASSOFERRATO: *Madonna of the Rosary*. Rome, S.Sabina

Sacchi's revenge came by way of his chief pupil, Carlo Maratta, whose extrovert temperament enabled him to take the leading position which Sacchi's shyness denied him: but there is good evidence that, during the 1640's, while Pietro da Cortona was in Florence, it was the classical wing of the Baroque which received the best commissions.

Giovanni Battista Salvi, known as *il Sassoferrato* (1609–1685), whose training is unknown, but whose style goes back to Domenichino—and even to the Quattrocento—was popular in devotional circles during this decade. His ceiling in the

52. SASSOFERRATO: *The Nativity*. Naples, Gallery

sacristy of S. Francesco di Paola dates from 1641, and the *Madonna del Rosario* (fig.51) in S. Sabina from 1643. The devotional feeling in these works, which is separated from the insipid only by a narrow margin, indicates a strong current of conservative taste which was tired of Baroque movement, and the enormous number of replicas (many of them original) of half a dozen of Sassoferrato's small *Madonna* designs indicates their popularity. In a picture such as the *Nativity* (fig.52) at Naples, the mood has something of the directness of the religious feeling of a late Caravaggio (cf. fig.24), although it is overlaid with a certain prettiness.

53. SASSOFERRATO:
Portrait of Monsignor Ottaviano Prati.
Rome, Galleria Nazionale

As a portrait painter of ecclesiastics, in a tradition deriving from Scipione Pulzone, Sassoferrato was also eminent, as the *Monsignor Ottaviano Prati* (fig.53) in the Galleria Nazionale shows. It is probable that his art represents a healthy survival of the purest tradition of the early Counter-Reformation.

Parallel with Sassoferrato is Giacinto Gimignani (1611–1681), a Tuscan from Pistoja, who achieved a rather more sophisticated variant of the same style and received a number of church commissions in Rome in the 1640's. His *Adoration of the Kings* (fig.54) at Burghley House, of 1641, is a particularly good example, with some relation to Romanelli, but significantly close to a work of the same date by Cantarini at Bologna (fig.87).

7 : LESSER FIGURES OF THE MID-CENTURY

A FLOURISHING tradition of painting in a great centre produces original and distinguished work at other levels than history painting and religious art. One of the most lively strains in Dutch seventeenth-century painting derives from the Roman experience of successive generations of Dutch painters—Poelenburgh, Both, Berghem, Du Jardin and Adriaen van de Velde—but their best work was, in the main, done after they had left Rome for their native Netherlands. But there was good patronage for popular genre in Rome, and the tradition of low life painting, begun by Caravaggio, bore fruit in the 1630's and 1640's in a class of picture which was called the *Bambocciata*. Bamboccio (which means something like 'silly great baby') was the nickname of Pieter van Laer (1592–1642), who was in Rome from 1625 to the end of the 1630's and created the popular picture of the daily life of the common people of Rome, which—to the annoyance of the practitioners of high art— soon had a substantial vogue. One of his largest and most lively pictures is the *Carnival at Rome* (fig.55; Wadsworth Atheneum, Hartford), which provides—in Passeri's words—an 'open window' on the Roman scene, which we are in danger of forgetting by concentrating on high art. The Fleming Jan Miel (1599–1663) carried on this style for the decade following 1636.

54. GIACINTO GIMIGNANI: *The Adoration of the Kings.*
Burghley House, Marquess of Exeter

55. PIETER VAN LAER: *Carnival at Rome.* Hartford, Conn., Wadsworth Atheneum

56. GASPARD POUSSIN and PIETRO TESTA: *The Vision of Basilides*. Rome, S.Martino ai Monti

'Ideal landscape', in the tradition laid down by Annibale Carracci and Domenichino, was probably considered a branch of high art, but its greatest masters,
Nicolas Poussin and Claude, although Rome was their theatre, are traditionally considered as part of the French school. Less meditated landscapes, however, with
specific reference to the picturesque grandeurs of the Roman Campagna, were held
to belong to an inferior class, and the great master of these was Gaspard Dughet
(1615–1675), brother-in-law of the great Poussin, who is generally known as
Gaspard Poussin. Dughet was a landscape 'specialist' and is recorded as having
painted his pictures with remarkable speed and none of Nicolas's laboured medita-
tion, but they are none the less charming for that. To the foreign traveller—and
especially to the English visitor—they set the tone for what a picturesque landscape
should be, and they were avidly collected. But he also collaborated with other painters

57. GASPARD POUSSIN and PIER FRANCESCO MOLA: *S. John Baptist*. Milan, Brera

in certain public commissions, and it seems permissible to detect, around the middle
of the century, a team of painters of real distinction who collaborated together just
below the level of the great commissions. They were also probably cheaper. About
1647/51 Dughet collaborated with Pietro Testa (1607/11-1650)—an engraver of
brilliant, if neurotic gifts, who never quite made the grade as a major painter—in a
series of frescoes in S. Martino ai Monti (fig.56), in which some of the abstruser
stories of the Carmelite legend are illustrated by small figures amid Dughet's ample
landscapes: and, about ten years later, Dughet provided a romantic woodland
background to Mola's *S. John Baptist* (fig.57; Milan, Brera) which was commissioned by Cardinal Omodei (Cardinal in 1652) for S. Maria alla Vittoria in Milan.

58. PIER FRANCESCO MOLA: *Joseph and his Brethren*. Rome, Quirinal

Pier Francesco Mola (1612–1666) just fails to be a major figure in the Roman school. He was a native of the Canton Ticino and received early training in Rome, which was supplanted by later experience of early Guercino and the Venetian school in North Italy. He finally settled in Rome about 1647, but his fundamentally romantic style never quite came to terms with official patronage. His *Barbary Pirate* of 1650 (fig.59; Paris, Louvre) is a splendid picture, half way between Guercino and Ribera, and he produced many minor works of great charm, especially of Hermits in romantic Venetian landscapes. In 1657 he painted his lovely *S. Bruno* for the Chigi, and, in the same year, he received his major official commission for the fresco of *Joseph and his brethren* (fig.58) for the Quirinal, but, although fine, it keeps uneasy company with the works of the lesser Cortoneschi which are its companions. He was official painter in Prince Pamphily's household for a number of years, but a quarrel in 1661 led to the destruction of what might well have been his

59. PIER FRANCESCO MOLA: *A Barbary Pirate*. Paris, Louvre

60. COZZA: Ceiling of the Library of the Collegio Innocenziano, Rome

masterpiece in the Palazzo Doria at Valmontone. He was replaced by the more docile and archaizing figure of Francesco Cozza (1605–1682), a pupil of Domenichino, who achieved poetry in his now almost invisible frescoes of the *Element of Fire* (1658/61) at Valmontone, but something like decorative nonsense in his enormous frescoed ceiling (1666/72) for the Library of the Collegio Innocenziano. In spite of the charm of many of the single figures in this busy ceiling (fig.60), it makes plainer than any other work of the period that the fire of the first Baroque had been spent and that the academic tradition was in the doldrums. Both styles were soon to be revived, but, as the academic tradition was to be victorious in the end, it will be better to consider Late Baroque first.

8 : LATE BAROQUE: BACICCIA TO FRATEL POZZO

IN the Cornaro chapel in S. Maria della Vittoria, with its altar of S. Teresa (1647/52), Bernini had provided the first major example of the conflation of painting and stucco with real and simulated architecture. The eye was meant to be deceived and to accept the illusionist convention that the architecture merged into the painted or half-painted heaven of the ceiling. This was to become the principle of Roman Late Baroque painting, which is primarily a style for dealing with the upper areas of churches—the ceiling of the nave, the dome and pendentives, the semidome of the apse were all to fuse together as a heavenly continuation of the structure of the church below. After the first great experiment by Baciccia in the Gesù, it was the *general effect* that came to matter rather than the superior quality of the draughtsmanship or of the expression of the individual figures: and, in the ultimate expansion of this style to Germany and Austria, where it reached its final flowering, effects of breathtaking virtuosity and beauty were achieved by painters whose names are little remembered because their work hardly stands up at all to a cool and rational scrutiny.

But the first Roman master of this style was markedly superior to his successors. He was Giovanni Battista Gaulli (1639–1709), known as Baciccia, a precocious Genoese, who had learned from Van Dyck and Strozzi to become a much livelier portrait painter than his Roman contemporaries. He settled in Rome in 1657 and he painted portraits of all seven Popes from Alexander VII to Clement XI as well as 'all the Cardinals'. The *Clement IX* of c. 1667 (fig.61; Rome, Galleria Nazionale) is a typically admirable example. But, under the influence of Bernini, who befriended and profoundly influenced a talent he found sympathetic to his own, he was soon receiving important religious commissions. It was doubtless on Bernini's advice that he visited Parma in 1669, to study Correggio, when he was engaged on his first frescoes, the pendentives (with figures of the *Christian Virtues*) for S. Agnese a

61. BACICCIA: *Portrait of Pope Clement IX.*
Rome, Galleria Nazionale

Piazza Navona (1668/71). These are masterpieces of elegance (fig.62) which combine Correggio's feeling for feminine charm with lovely colour and the form and expression of Bernini's later style. On their completion he was recommended by Bernini to the Jesuits and he transformed Vignola's barrel-vaulted Gesù into a Late Baroque Church between 1672 and 1685 by a series of ceiling frescoes of remarkable brilliance. The transformation of the nave was the most ingenious (fig.63). The theme is the *Adoration of the Name of Jesus*, and this and the existing shape of the roof demanded to some extent the concentration of a frame, while the desire for illusion rejected the limitation a defined frame imposes. Baciccia elaborated Bernini's device of combining real stucco figures with projecting flaps of stucco which were then covered with painted figures. It is not always possible from the ground to be sure quite which medium you are looking at, and this assists the illusion that the heavens are opening and you are contemplating a celestial vision. But the great bands of gilt stucco which cover the rest of the vault resist the illusion. It is a fascinating and resourceful achievement and the chief monument of Roman Late Baroque, but it was no more imitable than Pietro da Cortona's Barberini ceiling, which was the great monument of High Baroque. After Bernini's death in 1680 Baciccia's talent flagged, and his later altarpieces, for all their virtuosity, have a bright vapidity which suggests Hollywood. His final huge fresco, of 1707, on the ceiling of the nave of SS. Apostoli, has a limiting frame and a design which is fundamentally classical, although it is tricked out with light effects and frills to give it the air of being Baroque.

It became clear that the future of heavenly illusionism lay in treating the *whole* nave ceiling as a single painted unit. Canuti (a Bolognese) and Haffner tried this with some success in SS. Domenico e Sisto (1674/75) by the Bolognese expedient of an elaborate *quadratura* setting—but this was alien to the Roman tradition—and the final solution was only discovered by Filippo Gherardi at S. Pantaleo (1687/90).

Filippo Gherardi (1643–1704) came from Lucca. With his older compatriot, Giovanni Coli (1636–1680) he was a pupil of Pietro da Cortona and the two then refined their style by visiting Venice and North Italy. Their joint style is a distinguished blend of Pietro and Veronese and can be seen on the compartmented

62. BACICCIA: *Temperance*. Rome, S.Agnese a Piazza Navona

ceiling (*c.* 1674) of S. Croce dei Lucchesi and in the Galleria (1675/78) of the Palazzo Colonna. But Gherardi's masterpiece was done after Coli's death and is the *Triumph of the Name of Mary* (fig.64) which covers the whole ceiling of the small church of S. Pantaleo. The nave is of two bays, with a half bay at either end, and the ceiling embraces all. The arches above the windows curve in and are made to play a part in the illusion, reducing the opening in the ceiling through which the

63. BACICCIA: *The Adoration of the Name of Jesus*. Ceiling of the nave of the Church of Gesù, Rome

64. FILIPPO GHERARDI: *The Triumph of the Name of Mary*. Ceiling of the nave of S.Pantaleo, Rome

65. FRATEL POZZO: *The Triumph of S.Ignatius of Loyola*. Ceiling of the nave of S.Ignazio, Rome

vision is seen to a more manageable area. Figures whisk in and out from the central framed area to the side spaces, and the decorative figures under the window arches are mysteriously and ambiguously combined into the whole illusion. The smallness of the Church makes the effect a success from any point at which one might reasonably be expected to stand.

This is not true for S. Ignazio, the vast Jesuit Church whose ceiling frescoes by Fratel Pozzo are at once the final point of Roman Late Baroque illusionism and the springboard for Austrian and German imitations. Andrea Pozzo (1642–1709) came from Trento and was trained as a painter in North Italy: he was received into the Jesuit Order as a lay brother at Milan in 1665, and he became a painter of altarpieces and a perspective virtuoso in the service of the Jesuits. His work of 1676/77 for the Jesuit Church at Mondovì is remarkable, but he is not a painter whose work one contemplates in detail with particular pleasure. He was summoned to Rome in 1681 and in about 1685 he was set to work on the frescoes in the huge Jesuit Church of S. Ignazio. The fresco on the ceiling of the nave (1691/94) is his only work that rivets the attention, but more by its vast scale and by the opportunity given to the artist to exploit his virtuosity in architectural *quadratura* than for any more humane virtues (fig.65). It is a work of extravagant, and rather enchanting, absurdity. From most points of view—and especially from the sides of the church—the effect is wholly unnerving. Columns fall inwards or sideways and the spectator feels as Samson must have felt after he had started work on the Temple at Gaza. But there is one point in the centre of the nave (marked by an indicator on the floor) from which all this nonsense appears in correct perspective—and the effect is extremely impressive. It is not a point at which the worshipper in the Church would naturally place himself, and one may be permitted to wonder if the Jesuits conceived this bizarre scheme of decoration as a lesson to those who were not altogether on the correct spot in their religious beliefs. It is understandable that this sacrifice to theory at the expense of common sense should have appealed to the German mind. It was in a printed letter to Prince Liechtenstein, the Austrian Ambassador, that Pozzo explained the ingenious and detailed programme of the S. Ignazio ceiling— which combines a Triumph of S. Ignatius with a detailed statement of the benevolent activities of the Jesuit Order throughout the world. By 1703 he seems to have been free of his Jesuit commissions and he went to Vienna for the rest of his life. His major surviving work there is of a secular character—the fresco of *The Triumph of Hercules* for the great saloon of the Liechtenstein Palace. His work in Rome provides a neat close to Roman Late Baroque, but it is not in the least in the Roman tradition, and, by the time it was completed Roman taste had moved away from the Baroque in favour of the ornate Classicism of Maratta, which was to lead on to anti-Baroque Neo-Classicism by the middle of the eighteenth century.

9 : ACADEMIC LATE BAROQUE: MARATTA
TO TREVISANI

BACICCIA represents the legacy of Bernini. There remain to be considered the successors of the other two dominant rivals of the earlier part of the century, Pietro da Cortona and Sacchi. Rather surprisingly Pietro's followers are of less importance. His only pupil of real vivacity was Guglielmo Cortese (1628–1679), known from his birth in Franche-Comté as *il Borgognone*, and younger brother of Giacomo Cortese (1621–1676), the Jesuit battle-painter. He emerges as an independent painter at the end of the 1650's, but his best work is in the 1660's, his masterpiece being the *Martyrdom of S. Andrew* (fig.66) over the high altar of S. Andrea al Quirinale. This is almost Venetian in colour and shows an acquaintance with both Baciccia and Maratta, hovering between the style of the two painters who were already emerging, at the date it was painted (about 1670), as the rival successors to Pietro da Cortona and Sacchi.

Carlo Maratta (1625–1713)—or Maratti—was a precocious talent from the Marche, whose art was formed by many years in Sacchi's studio. He inherited Sacchi's deep respect for Raphael, but without his master's sensibility or feeling of

66. GUGLIELMO CORTESE: *The Martyrdom of S.Andrew*. Rome, S.Andrea al Quirinale

67. MARATTA: *S.Augustine and the Child*. Rome, S.Maria dei sette Dolori

(76)

inferiority to his great exemplar. He also cast an eye at the work of Lanfranco and Pietro da Cortona, as his earliest work (around 1650/52) reveals. But more important for the eventual trend of Maratta's art was his friendship with Giovanni Pietro Bellori, a writer ten years older than himself, and the dictator of art theory of his age. Bellori was an antiquarian and a close friend of Poussin, and he wrote of those he considered the most important artists of the age. Significantly, although almost incredibly, he left out Bernini. He championed Classicism against the Baroque and it would hardly be too much to say that he formed the taste of his time. He had begun a life of Maratta, which he contin-

68. MARATTA: *Portrait of Pope Clement IX.*
Vatican, Gallery

ued to 1695, the year before he himself died, and he is little short of thinking that art had reached its highest point in Carlo Maratta. A great deal of the rest of the world thought so too in Maratta's lifetime—and for that reason, as well as others, he has suffered a very heavy devaluation. But his fame was not merely an aberration of taste: at his best he was an artist of great distinction, but the extreme popularity of his pictures—especially his *Madonnas*—led them to be copied so often that judgment against him is often made on the basis of works for which he was not responsible. For the professional copyist his Madonnas took the place which Raphael's had held before.

Of his earlier altarpieces the *S. Augustine and the Child* (fig.67) of about 1655 in Sta Maria dei Sette Dolori is a masterpiece in the tradition of Domenichino's *Last Communion of S. Jerome*. The sunburnt Saint in black against a summer afternoon sky is a splendid invention. The story is dramatically told, but without Baroque commotion, and the drawing and paint quality are alike admirable. There is still a good deal of Sacchi in this picture, and Maratta remained connected with Sacchi's studio until the latter's death in 1661. But by the time of *The Immaculate Conception* (fig.69) painted for S. Agostino, Siena, between 1665 and 1671, Maratta had found his own specific style, which changed little for the rest of his life. It is a style of impressive rhetoric, in which each figure tells effectively. The types are well selected and judiciously idealized: the colour is powerful and the allegorical detail broadly and simply expressed. We are prone to mistrust the 'grand style' today, and it produced a great many dreary pictures in the century after Maratta established it,

69. MARATTA: *The Immaculate Conception*. Siena, S.Agostino

but it was a distinguished invention. The contemporary portrait of *Clement IX* (fig.68; Vatican Gallery) of 1669 is an easier example in which to enjoy this public manner. Compared with Baciccia's portrait of the same Pope (fig.61), it is less intimate, but it is no less penetrating.

It looks as if, during the 1670's, there was a deliberate exhibition of rivalry between Maratta and Baciccia. Parallel with Baciccia's Gesù ceiling, Maratta executed from 1676 onwards the ceiling of the Audience Chamber in the Palazzo Altieri (fig.70) just across the street. The subject is the *Clemency* of Clement X (Altieri), and Maratta keeps as deliberately within his framework as Baciccia deliberately bounds out of his. In colour it is nearly as garish as the Gesù ceiling, but each figure stands out clearly from the others and the whole picture is 'legible'

70. MARATTA: *The Clemency of Pope Clement X*. Ceiling of the Saloon in the
Palazzo Altieri, Rome

71. MARATTA: *The Death of S.Francis Xavier.*
Rome, Church of Gesù

in a way that Baciccia is not. From 1674 to 1679 Maratta was painting for the Gesù
the *Death of S. Francis Xavier* (fig.71), and, at the same moment, Baciccia was
painting the same subject (fig.72) for the Jesuit Novitiate Church of S. Andrea al
Quirinale. The Baciccia, which is perhaps his best altarpiece, is mystical and

72. BACICCIA: *The Death of S.Francis Xavier*. Rome, S.Andrea al Quirinale

visionary, with overtones which recall Bernini's later sculpture. The Maratta is grand and ceremonial and a handsome history picture in the grand style. This was the last occasion on which the two trends of Late Baroque came into competition, for, by 1680, Maratta was universally hailed as the greatest painter of the age.

73. MARATTA: *Madonna*. Vatican Gallery

It is probable that the originals of Maratta's small *Madonnas* and *Holy Families* were charming, but most of the examples one meets with seem to be replicas or copies, and he is better represented in this vein by the enormous *Madonna* (fig.73) in the Vatican Gallery. This is just under ten foot high, but the design is sufficiently

74. TREVISANI: *Madonna*. Rome, Galleria Nazionale

concentrated to bear this enlargement very well. Painted about 1693/95 it shows that, by the end of the century—about the time of the beginnings of the *Arcadia* movement in literature—the trend had set in which was to lead directly to Neo-Classicism. After this Maratta's work is usually much assisted by pupils. They were numerous and later had successful careers of their own, but they are curiously lacking in individuality and add nothing to their master's repertory.

Maratta's successor in European fame was a painter of entirely different training, Francesco Trevisani (1656–1746), who came to Rome with a Venetian background in 1681. His public commissions begin about 1695, just as Maratta's hand was beginning to flag. He excelled in all the fields Maratta exploited, altarpieces, mythologies, portraits, and, above all, Madonnas and small pictures of intimate devotion. But a much greater number of Trevisani's small pictures appear to be by his own hand. The *Madonna reading, with the sleeping Child* (fig.74; Rome, Galleria Nazionale) is one of the most attractive. The figure style has affinities with Solimena, and, during the earlier eighteenth century Academic Baroque became something of an international style.

75. ANNIBALE CARRACCI: *A Butcher's Shop*. Oxford, Christ Church

BOLOGNA: EMILIA AND THE ROMAGNA

THROUGHOUT the seventeenth century the broad tract of country which lies
between the Po and the Apennines, stretching from Piacenza in the West to the sea
at Rimini, accepted the artistic leadership of Bologna. Only at Parma and at Ferrara
are there to be found, fairly early in the century, a few independent painters who
cannot strictly be said to belong to the Bolognese school—and that means to the
School of the Carracci.

There were three Carracci: Ludovico (1555–1619), and his two cousins, who
were brothers, Agostino (1557–1602) and Annibale (1560–1609). At some date in
the middle of the 1580's they jointly founded a teaching Academy which they called
the Accademia degli Incamminati (which may perhaps be translated as 'Pro-
gressives') in reaction against the prevailing insipidity of the Bolognese Mannerist
tradition in which they had been brought up. Perhaps the most important tenet of
their teaching was the stress laid on naturalistic drawing from the model. All three
were beautiful draughtsmen, and they trained a remarkable number of pupils whose
drawings continue to give pleasure, even though the finished paintings of many of
them are often tedious. In the pursuit of 'nature' as opposed to the 'Idea' of the
Mannerists, they were no respecters of subject matter, and Annibale gave the
impulse to the genre which we now call 'caricature' almost by the way. The most
impressive example of this down-to-earth naturalism is *The Butcher's shop* (Christ
Church, Oxford; fig.75), probably by Annibale rather than Agostino and to be
dated in the earlier 1580's. There are the elements of a private joke about this
picture, since Ludovico's father was a butcher, and it is likely that members of the
family are represented. The broad handling and the realism (which is fully as
remarkable as that of Caravaggio) must be remembered as the background from
which Annibale later developed his extremely refined and classical style. The three
Carracci worked jointly on fresco cycles in the Palazzo Fava, Bologna (1584), and
the Palazzo Magnani (between 1588 and 1591), but their main output was of single
altarpieces in which their diverging personal styles can be discerned. By 1590 each
of them had separately undergone the experience of Correggio at Parma and of the
great Venetians, and the presence of Raphael's *S. Cecilia* in Bologna should not be
forgotten. All these influences strengthened them in their search for directness of
statement in the tradition of the High Renaissance and in opposition to the con-
voluted obscurity of Mannerist religious style. Since they sometimes 'quoted'
motifs or single figures, with brilliant appositeness and never slavishly, from such
earlier masters as Correggio or Veronese, the resulting style has long been called
'eclectic', which is only unjust if the word is taken (as it need not be) in a pejorative
sense. By the time Annibale left Bologna for Rome in 1595 (whither Agostino

followed him in 1597) the three had formed their independent styles, which appear
the more different the better they are known. After 1597 the School of the Carracci
is the school of Ludovico and is not quite the same thing as it was before: and
Annibale's final and classical style is a part of the history of Roman rather than of
Bolognese painting (see pp. 6–12).

What may fairly be considered the masterpieces (or among the masterpieces) of
the first mature style of all three Carracci can conveniently be seen together in the
Bologna Gallery. The *Madonna degli Scalzi* (fig.76) of Ludovico dates from about
1593 and shows to perfection the devout and popular style of the oldest and most
religious-minded of the three. The Madonna's head recalls Veronese, the Christ and
the S. Jerome Correggio: the comparative regularity of the general pattern is of the
High Renaissance but the irrational space is a legacy from Mannerism. Yet the
picture is wholly original and conveys its devout message with a tenderness and
directness of feeling which are combined with a mysterious visionary splendour by
the ingenious and irrational lighting. The silvery moon on which the Virgin stands
and the glory with a crown of stars behind her head (which ranges from pale green,
through primrose, to lilac) have dissolved or drowned any other colours. The
private mood of the two Saints is also very clearly indicated. In subjects which have
more narrative content Ludovico was less happy, and, deprived of the stimulus of
his cousins' rivalry, his later work tends to be tedious and to rely a good deal on the
older Mannerist tricks.

Agostino's chief contribution to the school was in the field of engraving and he
was also the most literary-minded of the three—and possibly the best teacher. His
pictures are rather few but the *Assumption* (fig.77) at Bologna, of about 1592/93,
finely illustrates how much he had absorbed from several years in Venice where he
engraved a number of the major works of both Veronese and Tintoretto. This is a
picture with clear, strong, local colour in the Venetian tradition: it is a continuation
of the art of Veronese with a strong vertical general movement very different from
the complicated diagonals which Annibale introduces into his own Assumptions
of more or less the same date. It is also much looser and less compact in design than
Annibale, who can perhaps best be seen, in his mature Bolognese phase, in the
Madonna with six Saints (fig.78) from S. Ludovico in Bologna and now in the
Gallery. Its date is perhaps about 1588. Here one is struck at once by the very compact arrangement of the Saints, in a perfectly rationally conceived space, which is at
times achieved at the risk of awkwardness (the figures kneeling uncomfortably on
the edges of the marble slab). Several of the motives are taken from Correggio: the
sombre twilit tone owes most to Venice and a good deal to late Titian: the rationally
ordered and balanced design is in the Central Italian tradition of the High Renaissance: and the emotional rhetoric of the Saints is already Baroque. There is no
doubt that Annibale was the great master among the three Carracci, and it is not

76. LUDOVICO CARRACCI: *Madonna degli Scalzi*. Bologna, Galleria

surprising that, after he was summoned to Rome in 1595 by Cardinal Odoardo Farnese, he should soon have been followed by the best of the school's pupils, Domenichino, Guido Reni, Albano and Lanfranco. It was Rome which enabled their art to expand into something more than a distinguished provincial style.

The mantle of leader of the Bolognese school after the death of Ludovico Carracci eventually fell upon Guido Reni, who only returned for good to Bologna in 1622, although he had painted a number of distinguished works for his native city

77. AGOSTINO CARRACCI: *The Assumption of the Virgin.* Bologna, Galleria

during the previous decade. In the meantime a new generation of painters had emerged in Emilia, all of them from the Carracci stable, but owing their individuality to contacts and influences outside the range of Ludovico's art. The greatest of these

78. ANNIBALE CARRACCI: *Madonna and Saints*. Bologna, Galleria

was Guercino, who will be considered separately, as his impact was national, or international, rather than local: the two considerable masters in the provincial Emilian school are Alessandro Tiarini and Giacomo Cavedoni.

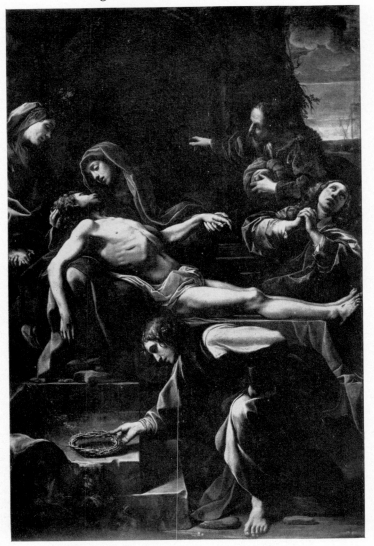

79. A. TIARINI: *The Deposition*. Bologna, Galleria

Tiarini (1577–1668) had spent seven years (1599–1606) with Passignano at Florence before he returned to Bologna, and Florentine types are still recognizable in the works of his best period, which extends from about 1615 to 1630. His heroic altarpieces, such as the *Miracle of S. Dominic* (1615) in S. Domenico, Bologna, and the *Deposition* (1617: Bologna Gallery; fig.79) are far superior in dramatic clarity to the later work of Ludovico Carracci and the *Deposition* may even have been designed as a Baroque and dramatic antithesis to the Neo-Classic quietism of Guido Reni's *Pietà dei Mendicanti* (fig.80) (Bologna), which had been completed in 1616. His major sustained effort is perhaps to be found in the series of ceiling decorations in

80. GUIDO RENI: *Pietà dei Mendicanti*. Bologna, Galleria

81. A. TIARINI: *Four Saints*. Bologna, S.Martino Maggiore

the Madonna della Ghiara at Reggio Emilia, at which he was at work for various periods between 1618 and 1629, but their virtues are more readily appreciated in a less ambitious work of the same decade, the *Four Saints* (fig.81) in S. Martino Maggiore, Bologna. The mood here is much more mature and subtle than in the earlier work, and the feeling for tonal values indicates that Tiarini had absorbed the best of the 'Lombard' tradition. His later work can be neglected.

Even shorter was the period of creative originality of Tiarini's exact contemporary, Giacomo Cavedoni (1577–1660), who came from the foothills of the Apennines, south of Modena, and must have added to the teaching of Ludovico Carracci a strong dose of actual experience of the Venetian great masters. This emerges palpably in a small handful of really distinguished pictures, all produced about 1612/14, of which the most famous is the *Madonna with SS. Alò and Petronius* in the Bologna Gallery, and the most original the *Adoration of the Shepherds* and the *Adoration of the Kings* (1614; fig.82) in S. Paolo Maggiore, Bologna. In the latter the splendid harmony of very dark blue, crimson and dull gold, with dramatic diagonal lighting, recreates the world of Veronese in 'Caravaggesque' terms.

Tiarini and Cavedoni at their best are dramatic painters, who take over from Ludovico Carracci a concern for the human moods and personal emotions of their figures. Their strength lay in representing the particular and not the ideal. The marble calm of classical statuary is not one of the ingredients of their style and their later falling off may perhaps be ascribed to an inability to adapt themselves to a

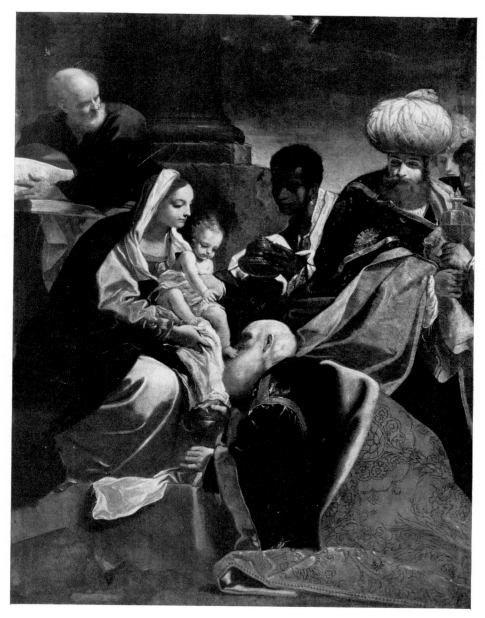

82. G. CAVEDONI: *The Adoration of the Kings*. Bologna, S.Paolo Maggiore

change of taste which was introduced into the Bolognese school when it became dominated by Guido Reni.

Reni's Roman work and the formation of his style is discussed elsewhere (pp. 13 ff.) and he had already executed a number of important commissions for his native city before he returned to settle there for good in 1622. The most illuminating

83. GUIDO RENI: *Samson*. Bologna, Galleria

of these is the *Samson* (fig.83) painted about 1611 as an overmantle for the Palazzo Zambeccari and now in the Bologna Gallery. In this picture the two strains in Guido's style are still to some extent at war. The dead Philistines in the lower right are shown with exemplary realism, and the twilit plain by the sea-shore, littered with the dead, although more poetically treated, is of the same order: the victorious Samson belongs to another world. He is an ideal hero, conceived from classical sculpture, whose pose, proportions and drapery are equally remote from any taint of realism. He might almost seem to represent Classicism and the ideal triumphing over Caravaggesque realism. The result is uneasy, but rather splendid. After he had finally settled at Bologna Reni's Classicism prevailed entirely and dominated the local taste. The most complete example is the great banner, painted on silk, of

84. GUIDO RENI: *Madonna with the Patron Saints of Bologna*. Bologna, Galleria

The Madonna with the seven Patron Saints of Bologna (fig.84; Bologna) which was executed as a thank-offering for the liberation of Bologna from the plague of 1630/31. The material on which it is painted gives a hard, cool, sheen to the surface, which is enhanced by the prevailing silvery tone. The handling is, in fact, notably broad but the strong lighting and the concern for outline give an appearance of porcelain finish, and each figure is strikingly articulate from a great distance—as is appropriate for a banner which was carried in procession. This picture set the tone in Bologna

85. GUIDO RENI: *Salome*. Chicago, Art Institute

for a decade and Guido's own personal development lies almost entirely in the exploitation of broad handling and silvery tone. In the two huge versions of the *Adoration of the Shepherds*, of which the finer is in the Certosa di S. Martino at

86. CANTARINI: *The Rest on the Flight into Egypt*. Milan, Brera

Naples, but the more visible (probably too closely visible) is that in the National Gallery, London, painted in the two years just before his death in 1642, Guido develops the logical 'old age style' to follow his earlier experiments. It is much admired at the moment (in reaction against previous dispraise) but I suspect that it is an utterance too large for what it has to say.

Rather unexpectedly Guido is in fact much more impressive in the few of his late works in which some ambiguity or subtlety of emotional expression is possible. Most of the pictures of this period depict rather blank figures which merely echo the very broad generalizations of his style. But the *Salome receiving the head of the Baptist* at Chicago (fig.85) shows how powerfully expressive this grand-opera idiom can be, when brought into sharp focus by the need for psychological refinement in the facial expressions. This is a most splendid example of 'the grand style' and explains the central position as a great master held by Guido, not only in the generation of Maratta (who learned much from him) but throughout the whole eighteenth century.

Of the artists who developed in the orbit of the later Guido Reni (and were at one time his pupils) the two most distinguished came from the Adriatic coast: Cantarini from Pesaro, which is actually in the Marche, and Cagnacci from Rimini. Both worked with Reni at some time in the 1630's, but whereas the short-lived Cantarini, towards the close of his life, showed the makings of a great artist, Cagnacci holds the attention rather as a curiosity.

Simone Cantarini (1612–1648) was one of the prettiest Italian etchers of the century. Although he seems to have had a turbulent personality, his best work has a reposeful devoutness which recalls a little that of his Marchigian contemporary, Sassoferrato. Although his outlines are sharp, his touch is always fairly broad and he has a feeling for tone values and twilight effects which owe more to Venice than to the artificial range of Guido. The *Rest on the Flight* (Brera, Milan; fig.86), perhaps datable in the middle 1630's, shows concessions to human feeling and a liking for sweeping asymmetry more Correggiesque than Bolognese, and a number of Cantarini's 'Holy Families' give one a nagging feeling that he had looked with profit at a Poussin of about 1630. Towards the close of his life he must have painted the *Adoration of the Kings* (Marchesa A. Torrigiani Salina, Florence; fig.87) which was the most remarkable revelation of the 1959 Bologna exhibition of the 'Seicento Emiliano'. This tender and beautiful picture is the work of a great master, not only of composition but in the handling of paint. In searching for a name to which one can liken the painting of the standing white Magus one even thinks of Velasquez. Cantarini died too soon afterwards for us to tell whether he could continue at this level of quality.

Guido Cagnacci (1601-1663), who was probably Guido's pupil a year or so before Cantarini, spent the last few years of his life at the court of Leopold I

87. CANTARINI: *The Adoration of the Kings*. Florence, Marchesa A. Torrigiani Salina

at Vienna. With Guido he abandoned an earlier inclination to 'Caravaggesque' naturalism, but he passed by Venice before returning to Rimini, and the two huge canvases painted 1642/44 for the Cathedral of Forlì (and now in the Gallery there)

88. CAGNACCI: *The Glory of S.Valerian*. Forlì, Galleria

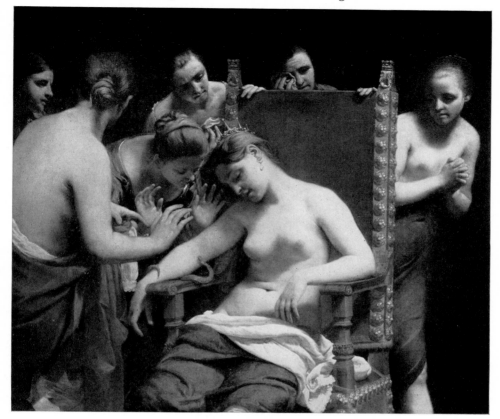

89. CAGNACCI: *The Death of Cleopatra*. Vienna, Kunsthistorisches Museum

would seem works of splendid promise if we had not now the foreknowledge of the direction towards which they were leading. The omens are clearest in *The Glory of S. Valerian* (fig.88) in which rather enticing nudes float swimmingly in a limpid blue sky, and youthful seminarists, seen in steep perspective, execute a charade below. The pictures are so wonderfully bright and gay that one is inclined to pass over the total absence of composition in the upper section and excuse, in the Seicento context, what one would find unforgivable in the art of Bouguereau. Of his later style at the Austrian court several works remain at Vienna, of which the *Death of Cleopatra* (fig.89) is the epitome. This cannot be denied the quality of being much in advance of its time. In this phase of his activity Cagnacci, at his best (as in the *Lucretia* at Lyons) suggests Prudhon, elsewhere Dame Laura Knight. Cagnacci belongs to the category of artists, such as Liotard, who paint with great accomplishment what is before their eyes but the poverty of whose imagination embarrasses the spectator. Compare the *Cleopatra* with Furini's *Hylas* (fig.137), a picture painted for the same kind of court taste, and the essential vulgarity of Cagnacci should become apparent.

A Bolognese speciality in the field of painting should be mentioned in passing since it is probable that, after the Carracci, it is what was best known about Bolognese art during the seventeenth and eighteenth centuries. This is what was called *quadratura* which means the art of illusionistic enhancement of space in the decorations of walls or ceilings. This was important or necessary in the art of the theatre, but the Bolognese exploited it in palace and church decoration to a degree unparalleled before—and Bolognese artists carried the tradition to many other Italian and Northern European centres. Their achievements, though highly ingenious, are perhaps not of sufficient importance that their names should be recorded in an account of the history of painting which is primarily concerned with humanist values.

Bologna was very active as a training centre for painters during the last forty years of the seventeenth century and all this artistic activity reached its culmination in the foundation of a professional academy, the Accademia Clementina, in 1709, but the leaders were men of feeble creative invention and their prescription for painting was the endless study and imitation of the works of the Carracci. In the direct line of descent were Carlo Cignani (1628–1719) and his pupil Marcantonio Franceschini (1648–1729). The latter almost vied in international reputation with Luca Giordano among those who preferred the genteel to the dashing. But the most agreeable of Franceschini's works are mythologies of small size which can be mistaken at first sight for works of the Carracci school of a hundred years earlier. Refreshing currents from outside Bologna can be discerned in the work of a few more lively painters, such as Lorenzo Pasinelli (1609–1700) or Giovanni Antonio Burrini (1656–1727), but nothing really prepares us for the emergence of a painter of real originality and brilliance, such as we find in Giuseppe Maria Crespi.

The work of G. M. Crespi (1665–1747) seems to be a deliberate reaction against all that was solemn and academic in the Bolognese tradition. He seems to have felt that a reformation was needed of the same sort that the Carracci had initiated a hundred years before against Mannerism: and he drew his inspiration from the same sources as the Carracci did—the great Venetians, Correggio and Baroccio—with one very important addition, the early, 'Caravaggesque' works of Guercino. In the field of subject matter he also may have derived inspiration from Annibale Carracci's early specimens of popular naturalism. In the 1690's he created a Bolognese rococo style of remarkable charm in some mythological frescoes in the Palazzo Pepoli, Bologna: and soon after 1700 he had established an international reputation for himself for easel pictures, often small, of genre subjects or mythologies. His altarpieces were mainly for the home market, but among the chief patrons for his more intimate works were Prince Eugene of Savoy, the Grand Prince Ferdinand of Tuscany and Cardinal Ottoboni. These genre pictures are freshly painted, sharply observed and entirely lack academic solemnity. A number of those painted

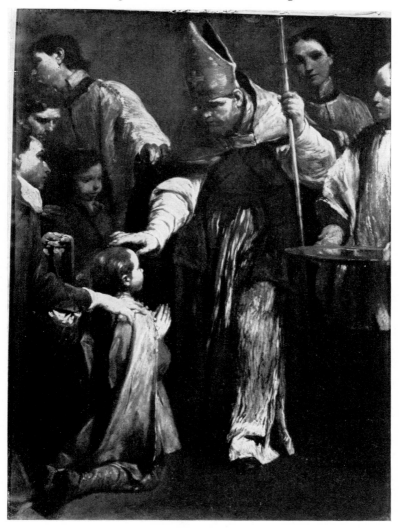

90. G. M. CRESPI: *The Sacrament of Confirmation*. Dresden, Gallery

for Ferdinand of Tuscany are still in the Florentine collections, but the most deservedly famous are *The Sacraments* at Dresden, painted for Cardinal Ottoboni about 1712. Among the best of these is the *Confirmation* (fig.90) in which the new taste of the age and the new pictorial resources employed to meet it can be excellently seen. In the Bolognese context its informality is specially striking, and this is enhanced by cutting off the figures at the edges in a way which reminds us of the camera or of Degas: the design is created by the light and shade in contrast to the linear methods of Bolognese Classicism: and the scene is one of intimate and domestic genre with equal emphasis on the personal character of each of the participants. It is not surprising that Piazzetta should have profited by Crespi's teaching.

91. G. M. CRESPI: *The Ecstasy of S.Margaret of Cortona.*
Cortona, Museo Diocesano

Crespi also applied this intimate, almost lyrical, method to his religious pictures. Although darkened and damaged, one of the finest is still the *Ecstasy of S. Margaret of Cortona* (fig.91), which replaced, at some date before 1713, Lanfranco's picture of the same subject (fig.34) in S. Maria at Cortona (now Museo Diocesano, Cortona). The quality of the Saint's ecstasy has become much more nervous: in place of Lanfranco's Grand Opera we are witnessing a scene of private alarm in which all the characters, Christ, the Angels, and even the Dominican dog, have the hallucinatory air of figures that one knows. The glimpse is momentary as if seen in a flash of lightning and we are moved as hardly before in Bolognese art. But Crespi's style was too personal (and his character too eccentric and isolated) for a school to develop from his art. His work is a last flash of genius in a dying school, but played some part in the broad European tradition which was to lead to the age of sensibility.

PARMA

FOR the decade of the 1520's Parma had been the theatre for the activities of Correggio, the most precocious of the great masters of the High Renaissance, who seems to us today to have been in reality a Baroque painter born a hundred years too soon. In 1545 Parma passed to the Farnese and the Farnese Duchy lasted until 1731. The Farnese rank among the great patrons of the arts in the sixteenth century and one might have expected that they would have fostered a flourishing school of painting at Parma, but it is only during the first two decades of the seventeenth century that the painters of Parma need detain us, though the genius of Correggio made itself felt throughout the whole of North Italy and on visiting artists from all over Europe until well into the second half of the eighteenth century.

While Cardinal Odoardo Farnese at Rome was employing Annibale Carracci on the Galleria of the family Palace, his brother, Duke Ranuccio I, sought to emulate the splendours of Rome and summoned Agostino Carracci in 1600 to paint in the Palazzo del Giardino. It is probable that the two most promising young native painters of Parma, Giovanni Lanfranco (1582–1647) and Sisto Badalocchio (1585 to after 1620), became Agostino's pupils at this moment. But Agostino died in 1602 and the Duke sent the young artists to Rome to perfect themselves in the school of Annibale. There they remained, working for Annibale and jointly producing

92. SCHEDONI: *The Three Maries at the Tomb*. Parma, Galleria

93. SCHEDONI: *The Almsgiving
of S.Elizabeth*. Naples, Palazzo Reale

engravings, until Annibale's death in 1609. Meanwhile the Duke needed a Court painter, and his choice fell upon Bartolomeo Schedoni (1578–1615), a native of Modena, who entered the exclusive service of the Duke in December 1607 and seems to have remained at Parma during his whole creative period of eight years, until his early death.

The little that we know of Schedoni before 1607 would not lead us to anticipate the way in which he developed into something like a great master during his few years at Parma. It can only be accounted for by something like the fulminating impact on a most sensitive nature of the art of Correggio. He produced a series of tiny pictures of the Madonna, which recapture a good deal of Correggio's sensibility and are lit in a 'Caravaggesque' manner, but his claim to our attention chiefly rests on a handful of large pictures which are either still at Parma or migrated with the Farnese collections to Naples. From some of these we can infer the influence of Ludovico Carracci and, in the *Almsgiving of S. Elizabeth* (Naples, Palazzo Reale; fig.93) we find a painter working in a manner parallel with the young Guercino, selecting his types with care and faithfully imitating nature according to the early precepts of the Carracci Academy. In the last two years of his life, however, he developed a manner which is altogether personal and original, of which the examples are the pair of pictures of 1614 in the Parma Gallery, the *Entombment* and the *Three Maries at the Tomb* (fig.92), and the unfinished *S. Sebastian dead* at Naples, which was found in his studio at his death. Just as the unfinished lay-in parts of the last picture seem to anticipate Delacroix, the *Three Maries* also looks forward to the age of Romanticism. A sort of mosaic pattern is made up of strongly lit slabs of brightly coloured stuffs or of flesh (lemon, violet and green are favourite colours); and the framework is made up of an intricate network of diagonal lines, which are dramatic and rhetorical as well as structural. It is a 'private' manner, perhaps slightly unhealthy, but unquestionably distinguished: and it seems to have exercised considerable influence on Lanfranco and Badalocchio when they returned to Parma after Annibale Carracci's death. Lanfranco stayed only a short time (between 1610 and 1612) and his subsequent career is part of the history of Roman painting (see

94. BADALOCCHIO: Cupola of S.Giovanni Evangelista, Reggio Emilia

pp. 40–46), but it seems to have been the combined influence of Correggio and Schedoni which reorientated his art towards the full Baroque. Badalocchio, a talented but lazy fellow, divided his time between Rome and Emilia and only settled at Parma about 1617. He is thought to have died young: otherwise he might have established a full Baroque tradition in North Italy, for his fresco in the cupola of S. Giovanni Evangelista, Reggio Emilia (fig.94), is a more remarkable reinterpretation of Correggio's at S. Giovanni Evangelista at Parma than that which Lanfranco, in 1620/24, executed for the Sacchetti Chapel in S. Giovanni dei Fiorentini at Rome (fig.35). The Badalocchio may well be earlier than the Lanfranco, which would indicate an artist of great originality and promise, but, after this remarkable beginning, the school of Parma fizzled out and came to nothing.

FERRARA AND CENTO (GUERCINO)

THE great age of Ferrarese painting, which owed a good deal to the inspiration of Ariosto, closed with Garofalo's death in 1559. In the same year the last of the legitimate Este Dukes, Alfonso II, began his extravagant and oppressive reign, which was made famous, or infamous, by the poetry and misery of Tasso. Soon after his death in 1597 the Papacy regained possession of Ferrara and conditions for serious patronage of the arts seem to have disappeared. At any rate the only two painters of distinction who were active at Ferrara during the seventeenth century were already mature artists at the time of the change of government from Duke to Papal Legate. These were Ippolito Scarsella (c. 1550–1620), known as lo Scarsellino, and Carlo Bononi (1569–1632). Bononi, whose chronology is unclear, produced a few altarpieces of real distinction in the 1620's, which probably owe rather more to the impression made on him by the much younger Guercino than, as has sometimes been supposed, the other way about—and Scarsellino emerges as the only really original and important member of the dying generation of the school of Ferrara.

Scarsellino's art develops in parallel with that of Annibale Carracci, but apparently independently—and without Annibale's Roman close. From Mannerist beginnings, in which Parmegianino was a leading influence, Scarsellino reformed his style with four years under Veronese at Venice and produced a handful of near-masterpieces in the last decade of the rule of Alfonso II. No nearer dating is possible. A few are altarpieces, such as the *Madonna appearing to the dying Magdalen* in S. Domenico, Ferrara, but most of them are small domestic commissions with mythological figures set in a romantic landscape. The best are in the Borghese Gallery, Rome, and the loveliest the picture generally known as *Diana and Endymion* (fig.95). In this there is something of the lyrical perfection of the *Aminta* of Tasso, and there can be little doubt that paintings like this and the best of Scarsellino's altarpieces counted for something in the artistic formation of the precocious genius of Guercino.

Giovanni Francesco Barbieri (1591–1666), known from a squint in his vision as Guercino, was a native of Cento, a small town in the duchy of Ferrara with no native school of any consequence. His emergence as one of the most famous, and also most admirable, painters of the Italian Seicento must be set down to the fact that he was a born painter with sufficient strength of natural genius to survive the conversion from a non-conformist to a conformist, which the prevailing winds of patronage demanded. No great painter is altogether self-trained in the technical sides of his art, but Guercino is one of those who formed a powerful and individual style through the sensitive appreciation of other men's pictures rather than through personal contact with a superior mind. A contact with Scarsellino has been mentioned, and one of Ludovico Carracci's finest altarpieces had been painted for the

95. SCARSELLINO: *Diana and Endymion*. Rome, Galleria Borghese

Cappuccini of Cento the year of Guercino's birth. He had studied also the frescoes of the Carracci at Bologna, but he had also grasped, by the time of his first emergence as an artist in 1614, two of the most important aspects of the Venetian painterly tradition—a feeling for the texture of the handling of paint, and for those strong contrasts of light and shade, in which the forms are partly dissolved in shadow, which is sometimes called *luminismo*. There is also a lyrical tenderness and delicacy of feeling about his small early religious paintings, which suggests a relationship, through Schedoni, with Correggio. By 1618 he was gaining considerable success at Bologna and he soon paid a visit of study to Venice: his first period closes with a summons to Rome in 1621 by his chief Bolognese patron, Cardinal Alessandro Ludovisi, who had just been elected Pope as Gregory XV. The most ambitious monument of this early phase is the *S. William of Aquitaine receiving the cowl* (Bologna Gallery; fig.96), painted in 1620. In a more romantic vein is the *Erminia and the Shepherd* of the same date (fig. 97a; Birmingham, City Art Gallery).

S. *William* is one of the first pictures painted in a stylistic idiom which can honestly be called 'full Baroque'. The spectator is emotionally involved in a fleeting moment of history, whose exciting content is concentrated on S. William's head, which is the centre of a swirl of movement, inwards, outwards and sideways. A sequence of discontinuous uprights at either side provide a flimsily stable architec-

96. GUERCINO: *S.William of Aquitaine receiving the cowl*. Bologna, Galleria

97. GUERCINO: *The Martyrdom of S.Petronilla*. Rome, Galleria Capitolina

97a. GUERCINO: *Erminia and the Shepherd*. Birmingham, City Art Gallery

Detail from fig. 97.

tural framework for this turbulent core, in which the forms are dissolved in a pattern of light and shade and the poetical significance of the scene is established by the direction of a glance or of an arm. It is a visionary picture of captivating originality. Compared with the work of the Carracci it can be called 'Caravaggesque'—but only if it is clearly understood that the art of Caravaggio himself counts for nothing in its origins. Guercino's assimilation of the Venetian and North Italian tradition was of the same order as Caravaggio's, but quite independent of it. It is necessary to introduce the name of Caravaggio, however, because it seems likely that this parallel development counted against Guercino's full acceptance by the world of fashionable patronage in Rome.

Guercino reached Rome in 1621 and he returned to Cento soon after the death of Gregory XV in 1623. In this brief period he was very fully employed and produced some of his most splendid works—the *S. Petronilla* altarpiece (fig.97) for S. Peter's (Capitoline Gallery, Rome), the frescoes in the Palazzo Costaguti, and, above all the frescoes on two floors of the Casino Ludovisi, of which the *Aurora* (fig.98), on the ceiling of the entrance hall, is the grandest. It is natural for us, as it was for contemporaries, to compare this with Guido's *Aurora* (fig.10) which had been painted only a few years earlier for the Casino Rospigliosi. The ingenious architectural framework was devised by Agostino Tassi. Its purpose is to assist the spectator in mistaking the painted ceiling for the real sky, thus giving Guercino's composition the effect of an exciting vision in which the spectator is involved. In the Casino Rospigliosi the spectator is merely looking at a very handsome easel picture which has been placed on the ceiling. Unfortunately the Casino Ludovisi is too low in height for the vision not to appear somewhat overwhelming. In spite of the airy lightness of the colour (all photographs of it are much too dark): of the romantic poetry of the figures of *Fame* and *Night* on the sidewalls: and such enchanting passages as the *putti* shooting arrows among the treetops: the whole composition is more a splendid wonder than a decorative success. The young Guercino had poured into it so much of the breathtaking power of his new art, that it seems to have alarmed the arbiters of Roman taste. It came a decade too soon and seemed to smack too much of those 'Caravaggesque' tendencies which were being routed by the prevailing tendencies towards Classicism of Domenichino and Guido. With the death of his Bolognese patron, Gregory XV, Guercino did well to retire to Cento and reflect on what he had seen in Rome and on the changing taste of the times. He had created a very popular kind of oblong historical picture with half-length figures: he had made for himself an international reputation—he refused, during the next few years, invitations to the Courts of London and Paris—and he carried on, for the next twenty years, an extremely successful mail-order business in large altarpieces from his modest native town. It took him some years to tame his art to the new fashion, but, by 1642, when Guido Reni died, Guercino was in a

(opposite) 98. GUERCINO: *Aurora*. Rome, Casino Ludovisi

99. GUERCINO: *The Cumaean Sibyl*. London, Collection Denis Mahon

position to move to Bologna and take over Guido's position as the grand old man of the Bolognese school.

There is a loss of fire, a movement from poetry to prose, in the works of Guercino painted after about 1627, when he completed Morazzone's frescoes in the dome of Piacenza Cathedral. His interpretation of religious stories becomes decidedly staid. But there is no loss of artistry: and, especially in his secular pictures of the 1650's, he attains a mastery of tender and tranquil colour which can only be fully appreciated when cleaning has restored his darkened pictures to their original freshness. *The Cumaean Sibyl* of 1651 (Denis Mahon, London; fig.99), with its wonderful harmonies of blue and cerise, is one of the most attractive. Compare it with the *S. William* and the conversion from the non-conformist to the conformist can be fully appreciated. But it is only when there is no story to tell, no narrative urgency, that Guercino's later language is altogether adequate.

VENICE

HISTORICAL reasons can account to some extent for the falling off in Venetian painting and patronage during the seventeenth century. The vast revenue which Venice had drawn from the Levant trade gradually ceased to be available, and she was involved in costly wars throughout nearly the whole century: the loss of Crete in 1669, after twenty years of struggle, used up her economies, and the temporary repossession of the Peloponnese at the end of the century was wholly unprofitable. Neutrality at home with hostile Hapsburg interests surrounding her was almost as expensive—but none of these things quite accounts for the almost total collapse of creative invention among her native painters. If we had only the native Venetian tradition to consider, it would be excusable, except perhaps in the field of portraiture, to pass over Venetian painting altogether. But Venice remained a great museum of her own High Renaissance painting and a place of pilgrimage for painters from all over Italy, and an inspiration to foreign painters, even when they were as great as Velasquez. Venetian tradition was one of the strongest elements in the revival of painting in the Carracci Academy at Bologna, and it was the visible works of Veronese and Bassano (and, to a lesser degree, of Titian and Tintoretto) which inspired a handful of Italian painters who settled in Venice, or left their works there, who prepared the way for the renewed flowering of Venetian painting in the eighteenth century.

The family studios of the great masters of the sixteenth century survived long into the seventeenth. Leandro Bassano lived until 1622: the last of the 'heirs of Paolo' Veronese (as they signed themselves) died in 1631: Domenico Tintoretto died in 1635: and Palma Giovane, the favourite pupil of Titian's old age, lived on until 1628. Palma Giovane was a considerable artist, but his best work was all done before 1600, and the thin trickle of respectable native painting does not derive from his teaching, but from that of a less direct follower of Titian, Alessandro Varotari, known as *il Padovanino* (1588–1648). It was from Titian's earlier works that Padovanino derived his occasionally attractive pastiches and this preference was transmitted to his four pupils who alone deserve to be named among native Venetian artists—della Vecchia, Forabosco, Pietro Liberi and Giulio Carpioni (1611–1674), the last of whom is an attractive etcher but a painter of very inferior quality.

Pietro Muttoni (1603–1678), called *della Vecchia* because of his gifts for restoring old pictures and imitating (or faking) their style, has two faces to his art. The three large altarpieces of 1654 in the Treviso Museum show his theatrical religious style, but he excelled in a vein which can perhaps best be described as 'Hollywood Giorgionesque'. A superlative example is the *Two warriors* (Sir Joseph B. Robinson collection; fig.100), in which a vaguely Giorgionesque motive is transferred from

100. PIETRO DELLA VECCHIA: *Two Bravi*. Sir Joseph B. Robinson Collection

the region of poetry into melodrama and dressed and cast accordingly. These Grand Opera toughs find their way also into della Vecchia's religious pictures, and it is some comment on Venetian Seicento taste that his pictures were not only much admired, but were even sometimes mistaken for the work of Giorgione or Titian. They are at least powerfully and unmistakably Venetian.

It is curious that the portraits of della Vecchia's almost exact contemporary, and probable companion in Varotari's studio, Girolamo Forabosco (1604/5–1679), should also sometimes, even today, be mistaken for the work of Titian, for Forabosco's talent was of a much more endearing and less pretentious sort. He deserves remembering for a single masterpiece, an enormous picture of a *Family miraculously saved from shipwreck*, of about 1670, in the Parish Church of Malamocco, beyond the Lido (fig.101), which is perhaps the most wholly delightful native Venetian painting of the century. It is light opera of a charming kind, in terms of Veronese: the anxieties of the various ages are excellently observed, and the modish mother's

101. FORABOSCO: *Miraculous Escape from Shipwreck*. Malamocco, Parish Church

Detail from fig. 101

scarlet shoes indicate the gaiety with which the party set out. The only casualty seems to be the hat which is being blown to sea at the left, and the intercession of the Saints to the Madonna in Heaven has a beautiful consistency of mood with the rest of the scene. Compared with this the pretentious Marine Venuses, and even the religious pictures, of Padovanino's most famous and successful pupil, Pietro Liberi (1614–1687), can be neglected. That Forabosco was the teacher of Gregorio Lazzarini, who was the first teacher of Tiepolo, is a link more curious than significant.

When we come to the painters from outside Venice who made Venice for a time their home during the seventeenth century, and left pictures there which played an important part in leading up to Venetian eighteenth-century painting, the roster is a great deal more distinguished. It is a curious fact, however, that, although we can detect something like a continuous development from one to another of the five most famous of these artists from outside, they do not seem to have met one another. It is rather that each was looking for the same sort of nourishment from Venetian painting of the past and took over the torch which had been lit by his predecessor. For each did indeed predecease the next. The first breath from the Roman world of Caravaggio and Elsheimer came with Carlo Saraceni (1579–1620) (see pp. 35 ff.), who was himself of Venetian origin but had learned his art in Rome. He can hardly have been back in Venice for more than a year before his early death and left there only the beautiful *Vision* of *S. Francis* (fig.102) in the Sacristy of the Redentore and a more ambitious uncompleted painting in the Doges' Palace. He was followed by Domenico Fetti, who first visited Venice in 1621 and returned the next year, only to die in 1623. After Fetti came Jan Liss, who may have met Fetti in passing in 1621, but only settled in Venice in 1624, where he too died, in 1629/30, just before the arrival from Genoa of Strozzi. Strozzi died in 1644, well before the arrival of Sebastiano Mazzoni from Florence, probably not long before 1648. Yet each of these seems to take over from the other in establishing a sort of underground tradition of Venetian painting which, although it met with little official approval at the time (except for Strozzi) seems to us today to be the true tradition which was to lead on to the future. It is above all a tradition in which the paint surface and the handling of paint is important and exciting—in which it differs altogether from the contemporary Bolognese tradition in which the paint surface is smooth and often uninteresting.

Saraceni must be considered as a Roman painter (see pp. 35 ff.), but we know next to nothing of the art of Domenico Fetti (c. 1589–1623), who was born in Rome and studied there first under Cigoli, until he went as Court Painter to Mantua in 1613. It was in Mantua, under the joint influence of the work of Rubens and of the great collection of Venetian pictures (that was soon to pass to England) that he formed the style by which we know him best today, but he must certainly have brought with him to Mantua a knowledge of the discoveries in landscape

102. SARACENI: *The Vision of S.Francis*. Venice, Church of the Redentore

103. PAOLO VERONESE: *The Flight from Sodom*. Paris, Louvre

104. FETTI: *The Flight from Sodom*. Sandon, Earl of Harrowby

105. FETTI: *The Blind leading the Blind*. Birmingham University,
Barber Institute

painting that were being made by Elsheimer. The comparison of Veronese's *Flight
from Sodom* in the Louvre (fig.103) with what Fetti made of it under the joint
inspiration of Rubens and Elsheimer (Earl of Harrowby, Sandon; fig.104) will tell
us more of the secret of Fetti's style than many pages of comment. He was rarely at
his best, except in a few portraits, in figure painting on a largish scale, as can be
seen in the many pictures from Mantua which are still at Hampton Court, but he
created towards the end of his life a sort of Venetian version of Dutch genre, which
was wholly original. A few of these pictures (notably three at Vienna) are Mythologies, but most of them are illustrations to one or other of the Parables: small
figures of genre character, usually in a landscape setting, beautifully and broadly
painted, which owes a good deal to the landscape backgrounds of Veronese. *The
blind leading the blind* (Barber Institute, Birmingham University; fig.105) is an
excellent example among many. And of each of these compositions Fetti himself

106. LISS: *The Vision of S.Jerome*. Venice, S.Niccolò dei Tolentini

painted a number of variations, each different in tone or shape. These are so numerous that they can hardly be altogether the output of his last three years, but they have about them something of the intense lyrical quality and nervousness that one has learned to expect from those who were to be overtaken by early death. They are a perfect blend of the Roman and Venetian traditions, but they look forward to a kind of picture which was to be developed by Northern painters (sometimes working in Italy) rather than to a true Italian genre. Fetti's successor in Venice was, in fact, a northerner.

Johann Liss (*c.* 1597–1629/30) was a German from Holstein who had been trained in the Netherlands and visited Paris before he reached Italy and passed through Venice in 1621 on his way to Rome. He was back in Venice by 1624 and died there of the plague five years later. His stylistic kinship with Fetti is so striking that it can hardly be accounted for merely by contact with the same Roman influences. Not only did he specialize in small-scale genre scenes with figures in a landscape, like Fetti's *Parables*, but he repeated and varied his compositions over and over again in the same way that Fetti did. His painter's touch is like Fetti's too, although he has a greater passion for curved arrangements and goes even further towards anticipating the style of the rococo. Mythologies, rustic genre and the more dramatic tales from the Old Testament are his favourite themes, but he was graduating to work on a grander scale at the time of his early death. The *Vision of S. Jerome* (fig.106), of which his third and latest variant was to be seen in the Church of S. Niccolò dei Tolentini in 1629, is certainly his masterpiece, but all his pictures can still give us the same sort of pleasure today. It is a pleasure in lovely crumbly paint, in the most complex organization of curved rhythms (S. Jerome's lion is especially striking), and in a lovely range of soft and tender colours. That this picture later influenced Piazzetta seems unquestionable and that it was etched by Fragonard seems equally inevitable. It is almost as remarkable a phenomenon in 1629 as Correggio's work had been a century before, but, in its own century, it seriously influenced only one painter, the Vicentine Francesco Maffei, who actually cribbed a figure from it.

In the time sequence, however, of these foreign residents in Venice in the painterly tradition, Maffei is preceded by Strozzi. Bernardo Strozzi (1581–1644), who belonged to the Capuchin Order, was a Genoese, and the formation of his powerful and personal style is a part of the history of painting in Genoa (see pp. 204 ff.). He was already under the spell of the great Venetians, especially of Veronese, before he settled in Venice about 1631, where he remained until his death. Unlike Fetti or Liss, who one thinks of as more or less 'private' painters, with a boy to help in the studio and little in the way of public commissions, Strozzi was in business in a larger way and turned out originals and copies or replicas of various degrees of authenticity, with the aid of several helpers. He was also one of the leading portrait painters in Venice and left his mark on the official style. His chronology during his Venetian years is inscrutable and there are no fixed dates, but he was almost alone in understanding how to continue the great Venetian sixteenth-century tradition and translate it into a Baroque idiom. The *Martyrdom of S. Sebastian* (Venice, S. Benedetto; fig.107) does this for Titian's (lost) *Death of S. Peter Martyr*, and is a splendidly theatrical picture, executed with wonderful energy and rhythmical force.

107. BERNARDO STROZZI: *The Martyrdom of S.Sebastian*. Venice, S.Benedetto

108. BERNARDO STROZZI: *S.Lawrence distributing alms.* Venice, S.Niccolò

Strozzi models forms with his brush in a way which recalls Ribera, as does also at times his selection of types as in the beggars in *S. Lawrence distributing alms* (Venice, S. Niccolò dei Tolentini; fig.108) a picture in which something of the lesson of Rubens seems to be incorporated with the more usual substratum of Veronese, a painter before whose knowledge Strozzi himself avowed 'one should bow and take off one's hat'. It is probable that Strozzi was the one important contemporary influence on Maffei and Mazzoni and the few painters of the next generation who matter.

109. MAFFEI: *The Glorification of Alvise Foscarini.* Vicenza, Galleria

Francesco Maffei (*c.* 1600–1660), though often attractively bizarre, is a painter of much less steady achievement than Strozzi. Trained in the provincial tradition of his native Vicenza (where the best of his earlier work is still to be seen), he was given his one Venetian commission in 1638 to finish a picture for the Church of the Tolentini, in which there were altarpieces by Liss and Strozzi. He worked always on the periphery of Venice, but matured his style by studying the great Venetians, especially Veronese, Tintoretto and Bassano. His best work all dates from the last ten years of his life, such as the *Glorification of Alvise Foscarini* (fig.109) of 1652 at Vicenza, which incorporates a figure from Liss's *S. Jerome*. From 1657 he lived at Padua and there produced, perhaps at the very end of his life, *The Israelites collecting the Manna* (Padua, S. Giustina; fig.110), a huge picture which is his most balanced and solemn achievement. His calculated asymmetries and often very elongated, almost Mannerist, forms place him a little outside the main tradition, but his imagination is original and impressive, and he is a master of both local colour and tone.

The last distinguished painter in this underground tradition is the Florentine Sebastiano Mazzoni (*c.* 1611–1678), who came to Venice about 1648 and died there, almost unnoticed, thirty years later. His two paintings for S. Benedetto of 1648/49 show that he had looked at Strozzi, but at nobody else in Venice, and, though confused as designs, include single figures which show flashes of insight in the interpretation of visionary scenes and are unforgettable. The peasant Madonna eagerly leaning forward so as not to miss what S. Benedict is telling her about the Parish Priest of S. Benedetto (detail: fig.112) is an invention in the spirit of Rembrandt, but Mazzoni remains a minor master, memorable for single figures of usually bizarre felicity. At his best, his visionary world has complete consistency and the *Annunciation* (Venice, Cini Foundation; fig.111) from S. Caterina makes one wonder if he had not seen a picture by Rembrandt and been moved both by his visionary lighting and his resolutely homely interpretation of the story. An angel, who is the reverse of celestially lovely and shows a great deal of knee, appears like a genie from a bottle and is glimpsed for a moment in a flash of lightning. If it is compared with the stately nonsense of Mazzoni's friend Liberi's *Annunciation* in the Salute, one can see all the difference between a private work of genius and an eloquent but empty public statement. Mazzoni's only spiritual link in Italy is with G. M. Crespi at Bologna.

After about 1660, and until about 1700, neither native Venetian painters nor resident foreign ones produced any work of the first distinction. The best new altarpieces were the work of the itinerant and almost international Luca Giordano from Naples, who either visited Venice or sent a picture there on separate occasions in the 1660's, the 1670's and 1680's. These pictures of Giordano (see pp. 192 ff.), of which the finest are in the Salute, provided the examples of standard Italian Baroque

110. MAFFEI: *The Israelites gathering Manna*. Padua, S.Giustina

style which were the jumping-off point for Venetian eighteenth-century painting.

Venice cannot be left, however, without some comment on her portraiture, in which her native painters were more experimental than they were in religious or historical pictures. Although the tradition of the Tintoretto and Bassano studios lingered on, it was a pupil of Leandro Bassano, Tiberio Tinelli (1586–1638), who, towards the end of his life, broke away from the Renaissance tradition, under the influence of Van Dyck's Genoese portraits. His portrait of 1637 at Hartford of

111. MAZZONI: *The Annunciation*. Venice, Fondazione Cini

112. MAZZONI: *Madonna* (detail). Venice, S.Benedetto

113. BOMBELLI: *Portrait of Paolo Querini*. Venice, Querini-Stampalia Gallery

114. TINELLI: *Portrait of Antonio Viari*. Hartford, Conn., Wadsworth Atheneum

Marcantonio Viari (fig.114) is one of the earliest examples of the satisfactory blend of Italian and Northern tradition in the field of portraiture, and a similar tendency, though less completely resolved, is found in the portraits of Fetti and of Strozzi. In the middle of the century there are only the clever pastiches of Titian produced by Forabosco, but Sebastiano Bombelli (1635–c. 1716) became the creator of a new style. He had studied at Bologna and at Florence before settling in Venice in 1663, and he introduced a new intimacy in his treatment of the head, which he was able at times to combine with the ornamental elegance of the Baroque full length. The best example is the *Paolo Querini* of about 1685 (Venice, Galleria Querini-Stampalia; fig.113), in which the unofficial intimacy of the head is in striking contrast with the formality of the rest. It was Bombelli who was the teacher of Fra Galgario (see pp. 145 ff.), who was to be one of the earliest portrait painters of modern man in his capacity as a private individual.

MILAN AND LOMBARDY

THE Duchy of Milan extended rather more to the West, into what is now Piedmont, than the province of Lombardy does today. For the purposes of the history of art it may be taken as embracing the more or less autonomous Valsesia, the alpine valley in which several of the most distinguished 'Lombard' artists were born and did some of their best work. It was controlled by a Spanish Governor from 1535 until 1706, when Lombardy fell under Austrian rule, but the affinities of painting in Milan with Spanish art, although they can be detected in the work of Daniele Crespi, are elusive and quite independent of those that are found in Spanish Naples. The most lively influence on painting in these regions during the later sixteenth century was that of the Valsesian artist Gaudenzio Ferrari (d. 1546), who had created, in the earlier of the Chapels on the Sacro Monte above Varallo, a new kind of dramatic religious art, in which painting was combined with realistic sculpture to effect a series of *tableaux vivants*. This tradition, which was as far removed as possible from fashionable Mannerism, was to survive in the rural sanctuaries of Lombardy right through the seventeenth century, and was to provide the strongest influence on the art of Morazzone and Tanzio da Varallo.

In Milan itself the direction taken by the arts owes a great deal to the powerful and noble personality of S. Charles Borromeo, Archbishop of Milan from 1561 to 1584. He initiated a series of new churches and charitable institutions in the city, whose artistic adornment he controlled on the strictest Counter-Reformation principles; and his heroic conduct during the plague of 1576 established him as a Saint in the hearts of the Milanese in his own lifetime. He was canonized in 1610 and his life and miracles were to provide one of the most inspiring themes for Lombard painters during the first half of the seventeenth century. His patronage and directive interest in the arts were carried on by his cousin, Cardinal Federico Borromeo, Archbishop of Milan from 1594 until his death in 1631. Milanese painting, during the seventeenth century, only rose above mediocrity during what has rightly been called 'the Borromeo period', and its solemn and rather passionate tone, perhaps tinged a little with Spanish gravity, is a direct reflection of the spirit of Federico Borromeo. He not only wrote a dogmatic treatise *De pictura sacra*, but he founded the Ambrosiana Library and presented to it in 1618 the first collection of pictures destined for public exhibition, and soon afterwards he established in Milan a (rather short-lived) Academy of Art.

The greatest of the artists of the Borromeo period, and so recognized by his contemporaries, was Giovanni Battista Crespi, known as *il Cerano* (1575/76–1632). By about 1595 he had returned to Milan from a period of study in Rome, where he had clearly been impressed by the latest work of Cesari d'Arpino, such as the frescoes of 1592 in the Olgiati Chapel in S. Prassede. He never abandoned the

115. CERANO: *S.Ambrose baptizing S.Augustine*. Milan, S.Marco

formulas of late Mannerist composition, but the bent of his mind was towards the dramatic and emotional interpretation of his subject matter, so that he never falls into Mannerist obscurity. In 1602/3 he painted four of the large temperas of the *Life of S. Charles Borromeo*, which can only be seen during the week preceding the Saint's Feast (4 November), when they are annually displayed in Milan Cathedral. These are scenes of nearly contemporary history, illustrated with remarkable power and originality, which may owe something to a knowledge of Veronese. But his masterpiece is the enormous *Baptism of S. Augustine* of 1618 (Milan, S. Marco; fig.115). Here the colossal foreground figures (well over life-size) are a standard Mannerist device, but the frivolous and ornamental character which such figures normally take on in a Mannerist picture is transcended by their solemnity and, to some extent, by their realism. The flickering pattern of light and shade is that of Cesari and as far as possible from that of Caravaggio: but the dramatic interpretation of the story is Cerano's own. This quality can verge on the melodramatic in the astonishing *Disobedience of Jonathan* in S. Raffaelle at Milan; or it can take on remarkable tenderness, as in the *Flight into Egypt* (fig.116) at Bristol, in which Cerano's rich and sonorous colour can be seen (as is hardly possible elsewhere) in its original purity. The intricate swirling composition of this design is a reminder that Cerano also executed designs for sculpture, of which the finest examples are the grisailles of about 1628 in the Museo del Duomo at Milan, which were later

116. CERANO: *The Flight into Egypt*. Bristol, City Art Gallery

rather feebly translated into stone for the five doors in the west front of the Cathedral.

About 1620 Cerano became *Principe* of Federico Borromeo's newly founded Academy, and it may be that the establishment of the Academy had something to do with the painting, at about this date, of the very singular picture (Milan, Brera) of

117. CERANO, MORAZZONE and G. C. PROCACCINI:
The Martyrdom of SS. Ruffina and Seconda.
Milan, Brera

The Martyrdom of SS. Ruffina and Seconda (fig.117) in which three painters collaborated. Cerano painted the left-hand portion: the rather invisible background figures are by Morazzone: and the lower right portion is by Giulio Cesare Procaccini (1574–1625), a sculptor-painter from Bologna, whose work is very extensively to be seen in the Castello Sforzesco at Milan. The contrast between the two main executants is amusing and instructive to observe. Cerano's figures are tensely emotional, rather sculpturally white, powerful in expression and beautifully modelled in the smallest detail: Procaccini's Saint is pink and softly sentimental and lacks any serious modelling. Yet the style of the whole is so overwhelmingly Ceranesque that we may fairly consider this a type example of the style of art which the Borromeo Academy was founded to foster.

One of the first of the younger generation of painters to enter the Academy was a kinsman of Cerano, Daniele Crespi (1598/1600–1630). He had a strictly Milanese training, independent of Cerano, but not uninfluenced by him, and he was extremely active in Milan and its neighbourhood from about 1619 until his death in the plague of 1630. He may have been more alive to the Spanish influence in Milan than the earlier generation of painters. The series of half-length Saints along the nave pillars of S. Maria della Passione at Milan (which is almost a Museum of Daniele's art) are like a more classicizing foretaste of Ribera's realistic prophetic figures in S. Martino at Naples: and one is reminded of Ribera (and in other places of Cerano) in the vast and impressive *Martyrdom of S. Mark* of 1626 in S. Marco at Novara. Yet these works are several years earlier than any paintings of this style by Ribera which are so far known, and, in his masterpiece, Crespi slightly anticipates Zurbaran in the same way. This is the *S. Charles Borromeo fasting in his study* (Milan, S. Maria della Passione; fig.118), which must be earlier by a year or two than Zurbaran's *SS. Thomas and Bonaventure* of 1629 at Berlin—a picture which set the tone in Spain for a new kind of pious history in which the Saint is spied on by the outside world. In Crespi's picture also two visitors are peering into the Saint's study and marvelling at his abstraction and at his austere repast of bread and water.

Crespi's last major achievement is the cycle of frescoes, finished in 1629, of

118. DANIELE CRESPI: *S.Charles Borromeo fasting*. Milan, S.Maria della Passione

119. DANIELE CRESPI: Frescoes. Milan, Certosa di Garegnano

Carthusian Saints and stories on the walls and ceiling of the nave of the Certosa di Garegnano (fig.119) on the outskirts of Milan. The arrangement of the fresco compartments here is still more or less in the Mannerist tradition, but the story-telling is direct and the series counts as the most impressive fresco cycle painted in Milan during the Borromeo period. Here too there is some affinity with the monastic style of the early Zurbaran.

The third of the triad of painters who had a hand in the *Martyrdom of SS. Ruffina and Seconda* (fig.117) was Pier Francesco Mazzuchelli, known as *il Morazzone* (1573?–1626). He must have been in Rome more or less at the same time as Cerano, and, though traditionally a pupil of Salimbeni, he too must have been profoundly influenced by Cesari's frescoes in S. Prassede. Indeed they form the basis for his fresco style in later years—and he is more distinguished in fresco than in oils. His early Lombard works are the elegant Mannerist *Mysteries of the Virgin* of 1597 in S. Vittore, Varese, but he only really found himself when he started to work in 1602 for the Sacro Monte at Varallo, and absorbed some of the dramatic realism of the style of Gaudenzio. Between 1602 and 1617 Morazzone painted two of the Chapels at Varallo, as well as one at the Sacro Monte above Varese and another for the Sanctuary at Orta. Many of his frescoes in this series are rather damaged, and the

120. MORAZZONE: *Ecce Homo*. Varallo, Sacro Monte

sculptures are the work of Tabacchetti and Giovanni d'Errico, but the combination of sculpture and fresco produces a dramatic *ensemble* which owes a good deal to rustic mystery plays. The *Ecce Homo* scene (fig.120) is remarkable because sculpture is involved in the upper tier of figures as well as in those on the ground. This is the genuine native art of rural Lombardy and it is a direct continuation of the local

Renaissance tradition and has a fine, healthy, distinction of its own and no parallel in the rest of Italy. In 1620, in the chapel of a 'Pia mortis sodalitas' in S. Gaudenzio at Novara, Morazzone produced a splendid series of frescoes, still arranged in more or less Mannerist compartments, and angels on the ceiling which are still strongly reminiscent of Cesari d'Arpino. On the side wall is a huge *Christ in Judgment* in the same tradition and of distinguished quality. Morazzone died in 1626 after having only partly executed the frescoes in the dome of Piacenza Cathedral, which were to be completed by Guercino. In the opposite chapel to that of the Buona Morte at S. Gaudenzio, Novara, he was replaced by a native Valsesian artist, Tanzio da Varallo (1574/80–1635), the brother of the sculptor Giovanni d'Errico, who had done the sculpture at the Sacro Monte for Morazzone.

121. TANZIO DA VARALLO: *S. John Baptist.*
Tulsa (Oklahoma), Philbrook Art Center

Tanzio came from the most northerly village of the Valsesia, and his first training was in the Gaudenzio tradition. But his rough Alpine realism had undergone an interesting transmutation in Rome, where he had come into contact with the Caravaggesque current at some date before 1615. In 1616 and 1618 he painted two of the chapels at the Sacro Monte at Varallo, where his brother did the sculptures. These are rather damaged, but he also produced a handful of very striking oil paintings, whose dramatic power has caused some of them to be optimistically attributed to Rubens or Velasquez. The two pictures of *David* in the Pinacoteca at Varallo show a wholly individual interpretation of Caravaggism, and the *S. John Baptist* (fig.121) at the Philbrook Art Center, Tulsa, Oklahoma, is a wholly original work. The alpine setting and the sculptural feeling of the figure show two of the sources for Tanzio's style, and the long and nervous fingers are almost Tanzio's signature. In the Chapel of the Guardian Angel in S. Gaudenzio, Novara (1627/29) he shows in the frescoes a greater power than Morazzone in the opposite chapel, and in the huge oil of the *Battle of Sennacherib* (fig.122), a rather hysterical masterpiece, he appears in the same relation to Caravaggio as Morazzone in his *Christ in Judgment* does to Cesari d'Arpino.

The plague of 1630 and Federico Borromeo's death in the following year seem to

122. TANZIO DA VARALLO: *The Battle of Sennacherib*. Novara, S.Gaudenzio

123. F. DEL CAIRO: *Salome*. Turin, Gallery

have brought to an end the period of real distinction in Milanese painting, which was not to rise again above mediocrity until the appearance of Magnasco at the very end of the seventeenth century. But the style of the Borromeo period was to exhibit a distinguished and neurotic decay in the personality of Francesco del Cairo (1607–1665), who fled from Lombardy, partly to avoid the plague and partly because he was involved in a homicide, and was established as a Court Painter at Turin by 1633. His *Salome* (fig.123), which is already recorded in 1635 (Turin, Gallery), is one of a series of tragic heroines who figure largely in del Cairo's work during his stay in Turin, which lasted until 1648. The passionate feeling and movement of Cerano has here fallen into emotional excess, and all del Cairo's swooning women and anguished figures of S. Francis awake in us the same sort of mood as a tragedy by Webster or Tourneur. They have the same sort of strong and heady poetry about them too. In his later years at Milan del Cairo falls off from this intensity and becomes, like the rest of his contemporaries, a bore.

PROVINCIAL LOMBARDY: BERGAMO
AND BRESCIA

THE most interesting painting in Lombardy after the 1630's was secular in character and the centres which patronized it were cities east of Milan which had long had their own artistic tradition. From the 1640's to the 1740's there worked at Bergamo and Brescia a handful of painters of real distinction. Though not linked by any ties of training or association, they have come to be known in recent years by the perceptive, if oversimplified, label given to them by Professor Longhi, of 'Lombard painters of reality'. Most of them painted religious works as well, but the bent of their genius was towards the portrait, still life or genre. Whatever invisible truths may have interested them, their method was based on the realistic treatment of appearances. The only Milanese painter of the beginning of the century whose style leads on to theirs was Daniele Crespi, who was in fact the teacher of Ceresa.

Carlo Ceresa (1609–1679) was probably in Crespi's studio at the time of the painting, in 1629, of the frescoes in the Certosa di Garegnano. By 1630 he had settled in Bergamo for the rest of his life. Since the time of Moroni (d. 1578) there had been a more persistent demand for portraiture by the Bergamasque nobility than obtained in any other Italian city. Bergamasque society was highly cultured, exclusive of outside contacts, and became increasingly tinged with Spanish gravity. Costume and formality moulded the character, and costume was mainly black and white. The portrait painter could only indicate character in these terms, which demand a nice sense of interval and pattern, and there is an obvious link between this type of portraiture and still life. Ceresa's masterpiece in this idiom, probably painted in the 1640's, is the *Lady with a white handkerchief* (fig.125) which has lately passed from the Sala family in Bergamo to the Brera, Milan. It is a study in black and white in which hands, face, and costume all count equally for the final effect.

A telling light is thrown on Ceresa's art and on the society displayed in his portraits by the work of another Bergamasque artist, who was almost his exact contemporary. Evaristo Baschenis (1607(?)–1677), in the intervals of his duties as a parish priest, created an entirely new kind of still-life picture. Although he also painted kitchen pieces, his main energies were devoted to arrangements of musical instruments, such as the picture in the Accademia Carrara at Bergamo (fig.124) in which the bulging forms of the lute, the mandolin, and the lovely new violins which were being produced at the time by the Amati of Cremona, play a silent music in which tones and intervals are most carefully harmonized. Such pictures are at the furthest possible remove from those displays of technical virtuosity in which Dutch or Flemish painters heaped food and fiddles in unseemly profusion. There is a gravity about Baschenis's arrangements which suggests the studious untidiness of a

124. BASCHENIS: *Still Life*. Bergamo, Accademia

cultivated society, and the musical instruments are treated with the same seriousness as the human figure would be. It is easy enough to discern a link between such
compositions and abstract cubism, and no doubt Baschenis was much concerned, as
all good artists are, with artful definitions of space, but I suspect that his pictures
always have a strictly humanist intention.

There is a great gap between the style of Ceresa and Baschenis, who died in the
1670's, and that of the other painters who have been loosely described as 'Lombard
Realists'—Fra Galgario, Todeschini and Ceruti. Their characteristic work hardly
begins before 1700, and reached its peak, as far as one can judge from the few fixed
dates which are known, during the second quarter of the eighteenth century. To
explain this gap one must postulate a change in the character of society in the North
Italian countryside of the same sort that was to occur, but rather later, in France
and England under the influence of the Encyclopedists and of humanitarian
ideas. In place of the closed, formal world of Ceresa's portraits, which was common
at the time to most of civilized Europe, we find in the portraits of Fra Galgario,
another Bergamasque, not only images of the smart and affable aristocracy of the
rococo age, but some of the first portraits of human beings as we almost know them
today.

Fra Vittore (in the world, Giuseppe) Ghislandi (1655–1743) was a lay brother in
the Order of Minims and is generally known as Fra Galgario from the Convent at

125. CERESA: *Portrait of a Lady*. Milan, Brera

Bergamo to which he was attached, and to which he dedicated the profits of a
remarkably extensive practice in portraiture. He trained himself on a study of the
great Venetians and then spent some years with Bombelli, and he did not finally
settle down in Bergamo to a very large practice until a little after 1700. He seems to
have had a genuinely simple nature, which put even the most fashionable sitters at
ease with him (though he avoided painting women as much as possible) and, in

126. FRA GALGARIO: *Portrait of G. B. Caniana.* Alzano, Canonica

later life, he ran a rather unruly studio and produced, as a very popular side line, a series of fancy pictures, using his students as models, often demanding to be given some such title as 'The young artist'. These anticipate the later genre of Drouais or Greuze. But his best portraits are of priests or professional men, mostly from the 1730's or 1740's, which can only be parallelled in European painting of the time by Hogarth or Chardin. There are good examples of all his styles in the Accademia Carrara at Bergamo, but one of the most remarkable is the portrait of the architect G. B. *Caniana* (fig.126), probably of about 1740, in the Canonica of the Parish Church of Alzano. A comparison of this with the Ceresa will show how far in the direction of the modern spirit portraiture had moved in Bergamo in the course of a hundred years.

This difference is partly of the same kind as the difference between city society

127. TODESCHINI: *Market Scene*. Montesolaro, Conte Radice-Fossati

128. CERUTI: *A Beggar*. Brescia, Salvadego Collection

and country life, in which the Italians have always had a genius for relaxation. It would seem (though this is guess-work) that a taste developed for having paintings in these country villas to which the landed proprietors increasingly resorted, and that, just as the Dutch furnished their dining rooms with paintings of vast masses of food and plate, the North Italians began to fill their villas with pictures of the low life of the countryside. So at least one would deduce from the survival in a few such country retreats of the few such pictures of this new sort which have survived more or less where they were painted.

It is not clear who was the father of this new genre, but it may have been Giacomo Francesco Cipper, known from his German origin as *Todeschini*, whose working dates, as at present known, are 1705–1736. A series of six pictures, commissioned by Conte Alfonso Vismara for his villa of Montesolaro in the province of Como is still *in situ* (Coll.: Conte Radice-Fossati), of which the largest is the *Market scene* (fig. 127). The steward is seen buying some excellent peaches, and there is a beggar in the background, and one is led to wonder whether the feeling of comfortable life in a villa was not enhanced by representations of extreme poverty in the countryside—for such was the speciality of the other leading painter of this genre, Ceruti.

Giacomo Ceruti (recorded working dates 1720–1750/60) was even known as *il Pitocchetto* (i.e. the 'beggar-painter') in the Brescian district where he worked. He painted a number of more or less fashionable portraits, not far in style from those of Fra Galgario, and a few altarpieces, but he seems to have filled the villas on the shores of Lake Garda and in the Brescian countryside with pictures of the dregs of rural life, such as the *Beggar* (fig. 128). These are works of genuine realism, observed neither with sympathy nor disgust. Their nearest parallel is with the works of the Le Nain brothers, of some eighty years earlier, which began to fetch good prices in France a decade or so after Ceruti. The taste for such pictures in a sophisticated age has never been altogether explained, but it may well be simply because the age had reached an advanced stage of sophistication that it liked them. They hardly connect directly with the works of the Bamboccianti in Rome of a century earlier, but rather represent a current of taste which is continually cropping up.

FLORENCE

THE artistic situation in Florence is much closer to that in Bologna for the last quarter of the sixteenth century than the general neglect into which it has fallen until very recent times would lead one to suppose. But the artistic personalities were a great deal less forceful than were the Carracci, and there was no consciously progressive stylistic tradition which produced a succession of brilliant pupils to carry further the advances made by the first generation who reacted against Mannerism. This reaction in fact occurs earlier in Florence than it did in Bologna, but in the mild personality of Santi di Tito (1536–1603), whose gentle and noble style in his best pictures won favour in many circles, but lacked the force of an opposition programme. His *Baptism* (fig.129; Galleria Corsini, Florence), painted about 1574, the year of Vasari's death, is a return to the clarity of the Florentine High Renaissance, and it might seem to look forward to a great development, but neither Santi di Tito, nor the generation of painters who followed him in the same anti-Mannerist path, ever went much beyond it, or followed up the lessons implicit in the occasionally admirable pictures they produced. The fault probably lay in the increasing provincialism which beset the Grand Duchy of Tuscany, especially after the death of Ferdinand I in 1609. For, though the Florentine Court was luxurious and extravagant, it lacked the metropolitan status which Rome could provide as a stimulus to her artists, and the Grand-ducal taste ran rather in the direction of expensive *bijouterie* and the commissioning of articles in *pietra dura*.

Of the three painters of distinction in the generation which followed Santi di Tito, Jacopo da Empoli (*c.* 1554–1640), Domenico Passignano (1558/60–1638) and Lodovico Cigoli (1559–1613), the first two hardly changed throughout their long lives from the style they had achieved by 1600, and they were far surpassed in power and originality by Cigoli.

One or two of Cigoli's pictures have been confused with the work of Annibale Carracci, and he ranks as Annibale's Florentine equivalent. Even the sources for his style are the same as Annibale's, for he learned a good deal from the Venetians, and he picked up from the study of Baroccio some elements of what Annibale had learned more directly from Correggio. In later life, too, Cigoli, spent a number of years in Rome with profit. His aspirations towards a new style are evident, yet he is oddly lacking in consistent development, though he is never banal. He was an architect also and a sculptor, and his remarkable sketches seem to owe a good deal to Tintoretto. In one picture of 1597, the *Martyrdom of St. Stephen* (fig.130; Florence, Pitti) he seems to anticipate the Baroque, and this painting was understandably much admired by Pietro da Cortona. Yet he made no further progress in that direction, and what is perhaps his masterpiece, the *Adoration of the Kings*, dated

129. SANTI DI TITO: *The Baptism of Christ*. Florence, Galleria Corsini

130. CIGOLI: *The Martyrdom of S.Stephen*. Florence, Palazzo Pitti

131. CIGOLI: *The Adoration of the Kings*. Stourhead, National Trust

1605, from S. Piero Maggiore, which is now at Stourhead (fig.131), is simply a very handsome example of High Renaissance style. In his powerful and moving *Ecce Homo* (fig.132) of about 1606 (Florence, Pitti), he clearly shows the influence of

132. CIGOLI: *Ecce Homo*. Florence, Palazzo Pitti

Caravaggio, in competition with whom it was painted at Rome: and, under the avowed influence of Baroccio, he painted a series of pictures of *S. Francis in Ecstasy*, which compare favourably with similar experiments by Annibale Carracci—but these pictures had no echoes in later Florentine painting.

133. CRISTOFANO ALLORI: *Judith with the head of Holofernes.*
Florence, Palazzo Pitti

Cigoli's best pupil was Giovanni Bilivert (1576–1644), a Florentine born of
Flemish parents, whose work is often of considerable distinction: but the painter of
this generation who occasionally surprises us by producing a masterpiece is Cristofano Allori (1577–1621). Two of his pictures in the Pitti, the *Judith* (fig.133) and
S. Julian welcoming poor travellers (fig.134), are the masterpieces of the Florentine
Grand Style and were long among the most admired pictures in Italy. The modern
preoccupation with the Baroque has made them unfashionable today, but a candid

134. CRISTOFANO ALLORI: *The Hospitality of S.Julian.* Florence, Palazzo Pitti

taste, which will trouble to look at them, will be rewarded. By contrast, the work of Matteo Rosselli (1578–1650), who happened to be the teacher of Giovanni da San Giovanni, Furini and the best painters of the next generation—which can also be seen at the Pitti—appears very pedestrian.

The Court's commissions to painters were principally for portraits from the Flemish Justus Sustermans (1597–1681), who was official painter to the Medici Court from 1620 until his death; or they were for works of intimate devotion, such as were ordered from Carlo Dolci by the Grand Duchesses, whose piety tended to border on the extravagant. Florence in fact became increasingly priest-ridden and the conservative character of ecclesiastical taste can be seen in hundreds of tedious altarpieces which show no awareness of Roman Baroque. The aristocracy, which was allowed no part in the administration, exercised considerable patronage of contemporary art, but its taste tended to be stuffy or esoteric. The voluptuous half-nudes of Furini represent the reverse of a piety, whose manifestations were very much on the surface.

The most agreeable aspect of Florentine provincialism was a liking, shared by Court and aristocracy, for life in the country. This is reflected in the best work of the one considerable native fresco painter, Giovanni Mannozzi, called Giovanni da San Giovanni (1592–1636). In 1621 he painted a small chapel, which has now been reconstructed in the sculpture section of the Istituto di Belle Arti. The compartmenting is still Mannerist, but the main scene, *The Holy family descending at an inn* (fig.135), is a work of the greatest charm which owes a good deal to its capturing this rustic air of Tuscan country life. It is noble in its main lines, but the reverse of solemn, and its virtues are of the lyrical or pastoral kind. It is also wholly original. Something of the same kind can be detected through a good deal of repaint in Giovanni da San Giovanni's portion of the frescoes in the Sala degli Argenti on the ground floor of the Pitti Palace, which were unfinished at his death in 1636, but for whose whole programme he was responsible. The elaborate painted architectural framework in which the narrative frescoes are set is provincial and unsatisfactory, but the decorative resource is considerable.

The rest of the great hall in the Palazzo Pitti was completed by other hands, and it would seem that it was not considered a success, as the Grand Duke employed Pietro da Cortona, who chanced to be visiting Florence, to paint the walls of the Camera della Stufa in 1637. But the two scenes by Francesco Furini (1603–46) are distinguished and impressive—especially the *Allegory on the Death of Lorenzo il Magnifico* (fig.136). It is not clear how far Furini, who did not normally work in fresco but seems to have had a natural talent for it, was following the indications of Giovanni da San Giovanni, with whom he had collaborated in Rome in the 1620's. But his colour is quite individual and his figures more dramatic than Giovanni's. He had clearly studied Raphael's *Stanze* with attention and the mourning River God owes a great deal to Andrea del Sarto, while the whole composition is based on an exciting spiral which makes it one of the few near-Baroque designs by a Florentine painter. In the more direct technique of fresco there was no room for the parlour refinements which tend to give too hot-house an air to Furini's later work. These

135. GIOVANNI DA SAN GIOVANNI: *The Holy Family arriving at an Inn.*
Florence, Istituto di Belle Arti

136. FURINI: *Allegory on the Death of Lorenzo il Magnifico*. Florence, Museo degli Argenti

137. FURINI: *Hylas and the Nymphs*. Florence, Palazzo Pitti

frescoes of 1639/42 are his only securely dated works, but it is likely that the large *Hylas and the Nymphs* (Florence, Pitti; fig.137) may be a year or two earlier. This somewhat theatrical masterpiece perhaps tells us a good deal about the private taste of the Florentine aristocracy. Hylas is in a bright and sinister red and the stormy sky is so dark that only a flash of lightning can have illumined the figures as they are. The poetry is that of Marino rather than of Tasso, but the nymphs are admirably drawn and arranged and there are psychological overtones in the expression on Hylas's face and in the insouciant quartet of nymphs at the right which indicate the nature of Furini's gifts.

It was not until the death of his grandmother in 1636 that the Grand Duke Ferdinand II had a fairly free hand, either in politics or art patronage, and it may be that his employment of Pietro da Cortona in 1637 for the Camera della Stufa (fig.138) suggests that he was trying to import the Roman style. Certainly he approved of the result, for, when he further enlarged the Pitti Palace in 1640, the adornment of the ceilings of the new rooms was given to Cortona, who was at work on them from 1641 to 1647, leaving them unfinished to return to Rome, probably because his chief patron, Urban VIII, owing to the war over Castro, was more than

Detail from fig. 137

usually at loggerheads with the Grand Duke. They were completed by his pupil, Ciro Ferri, who made Florence his home from 1659 to 1665.

Pietro da Cortona's rooms in the Pitti Palace set the tone for the official Court style in Florence for the rest of the century. He decorated, in whole or in part, five rooms named after the five planets then known. They are different in intention from his Roman decorations because the effect is achieved at least as much by the stucco ornamentation (for which Pietro was also reponsible) as by the painting. They aim at superlatively grand decoration rather than at an effect of power: they suggest wealth and luxury and a splendid court. The meaning in detail is not in the least clear to read (as it was in the Camera della Stufa), and they are more significant for the history of Pietro as an architectural decorator than as a painter.

138. PIETRO DA CORTONA: *The Golden Age*. Florence, Palazzo Pitti

In contrast to this Roman style for secular decoration, there developed in Florence during the forties an intimate devotional style of a very different character, which concentrated on small pictures, with relatively few figures—and all of these significant—in contrast to the riots which prevailed in Pietro's compositions. The

139. DOLCI: *Portrait of Fra Ainolfo dei Bardi.*
Florence, Palazzo Pitti

140. DOLCI: *David with the head of Goliath.*
Milan, Brera

situation is somewhat parallel to Sacchi's opposition to Pietro at Rome, although the protagonist, a far from negligible painter, must be ranked a good deal below Sacchi. He was Carlo Dolci (1616–86) and his best pictures were executed in the 1640's in a style closely parallelled by the High Baroque Classicism which prevailed in Rome during the same decade. In 1632, at the age of sixteen, he painted the life-size portrait of *Fra Ainolfo dei Bardi* (Florence, Pitti; fig. 139), a broadly handled master-piece on the scale of life, with the figure outlined against an evening sky, which is the only foretaste of the twilights he was later to prefer. Even as late as 1665/70, he could still paint portraits of unusual distinction as those of *Sir John Finch* and *Sir Thomas Baines* (Mr. Christie-Miller) demonstrate: but he was smitten with an obsession to paint only devotional works and seems to have lived at the mercy of his confessor. The *S. Andrew adoring his Cross* of 1646 (Florence, Pitti; fig. 141) is the most deeply felt of these and is interesting to compare with the same subject as painted by Sacchi ten years earlier. There is the same extreme care over the psycho-logy and precise movement of each figure in contrast to Pietro da Cortona's slapdash crowds. The small background figures and the landscape reveal a debt to Andrea del Sarto, and there is a feeling for tone in the picture (in spite of S. Andrew's very intense blue drapery), which is wholly admirable.

Something of the same quality on the scale of life is found in the *David with the head of Goliath* (Milan, Brera; fig. 140) which also seems to be dated in the 1640's: but Dolci later lapsed into a licked and polished technique, often on a copper base,

141. DOLCI: *S.Andrew adoring his Cross.* Florence, Palazzo Pitti

which made him into a sort of Florentine Gerard Dou. This was the unfortunate taste of that silly woman, the Grand Duchess Vittoria, doubtless in deliberate opposition to her husband's. She conveyed it to some extent to her son, Cosimo III, who succeeded Ferdinand II in 1670.

Dolci, for all his faults, remained in the Florentine tradition all his life. This was not true of his near-contemporary, Baldassare Franceschini, called *il Volterrano*

142. VOLTERRANO: *The practical joke of the Priest Arlotto*. Florence, Palazzo Pitti

(1611–1689). In an early work, perhaps of the 1640's, *The practical joke of the Priest Arlotto* (Florence, Pitti; fig.142), he produced one of the freshest and gayest Florentine paintings of the century, in the direct succession to Giovanni da San Giovanni's popular peasant tradition—but his later works are mainly competent exercises in the prevailing Cortonesque style.

It is curious that something of this native Florentine rural tradition should have been recaptured in the last major work of decoration to be painted in Florence during the seventeenth century—and that by the Neapolitan Luca Giordano. In 1682 he painted the fairly small Galleria on an upper floor of the garden courtyard for the Marchese Riccardi, who had acquired the old Palazzo Medici in 1659. The subject might have seemed worthy to rival with that of Pietro da Cortona's Barberini ceiling, for it was 'The apotheosis of the dynasty of the Medici and the advantage of their rule to commerce, industry, arts and letters'. The figure style is indeed very elegantly aped from that of Pietro da Cortona, and it is true that there is, in the centre of the ceiling, looking as though it was brushed in as an afterthought, a rather absurd 'burst' with a lot of Medici portraits. But the substance of the decoration is all along the cove of the ceiling (fig.143) round the edges. Groups of allegorical figures, widely spaced and easy to interpret (inscriptions below each *motif* explain the figures above) form a sort of frieze with the atmosphere of a picnic

143. LUCA GIORDANO: *Allegory of Navigation*. Florence, Palazzo Medici-Riccardi

on a summer's day. It is a lovely and rather frivolous room, in which, as in a return
to the spirit of the Galleria Farnese, the gold and white boiseries and mirrors on the
walls opposite to the windows play an important decorative part, but it lightly
evades all those implications of power and propaganda which are implicit in the
true Roman Baroque style.

SIENA

THE bloody history of Siena and her conflict with Florence came to an end in 1559, when the city and most of her territory were allocated to Cosimo of Tuscany by the Treaty of Cateau Cambrésis. But her artistic vitality and independence did not altogether dry up until the middle of the seventeenth century. Around the crucial decade of 1590–1600 she had two distinguished painters, half-brothers, Francesco Vanni (1563?–1610) and Ventura Salimbeni (1568?–1613), the former of whom at any rate, while always retaining much of the Mannerist scale of colour, painted a few pictures whose devotional lucidity and simple, but strong, emotional content provide a parallel with what Ludovico Carracci was doing at Bologna and with the best work of Cigoli at Florence. Salimbeni's work hardly looks forward to the Baroque, but Francesco Vanni's masterpiece (fig.144), the *Vision of S. Francis* of

144. F. VANNI: *The Vision of S.Francis*. Providence, Rhode Island School of Design

145. R. MANETTI: *The Rest on the Flight into Egypt.*
Siena, S.Pietro in Castelvecchio

1599 (Providence, R.I.), interprets a vision with a direct and striking realism, which justifies us in classing it as a Proto-Baroque painting. No doubt the strongest influence on Vanni at this time was Baroccio, and the unusual quality of the picture may be in part due to the fact that it was commissioned for a Chapel of the Franciscan Observants (at Lyons). This forward-looking phase of Vanni perhaps ends with his *Fall of Simon Magus*, painted in 1603 for S. Peter's at Rome—a commission which shows the esteem in which he was held at the time.

A pupil of Vanni, Rutilio Manetti (1571–1639), was the last Sienese painter of any real originality, but his most interesting work was done wholly under the influence of the Roman Caravaggesques. He seems to have painted some low-life pictures in the style of Valentin, but perhaps the only picture for which he deserves honourable mention is the *Rest on the Flight* (fig.145) of 1621 on the high altar of S. Pietro in Castelvecchio, Siena. This accomplished and original design has considerable affinities with the work of the young Guercino. Manetti's later work shows a falling off from this level and the taste of Siena became increasingly academic and Bolognese.

NAPLES

SINCE 1503 the south of Italy had been a Spanish province, ruled by a Viceroy at Naples, which was the headquarters of the Spanish garrison in Italy. After a period of baronial disturbance a settled court life had been established, perhaps the most opulent in Italy, by 1600 when the Royal Palace, the seat of the Viceroy, was begun. The ruling classes were overwhelmingly Spanish and their rule was the most oppressive in Italy: executions were of common occurrence and social conditions encouraged that double strain of cruelty and delinquency which is reflected in the art of the Spanish Ribera, the greatest of the Neapolitan painters of the seventeenth century, and has left its mark on Naples today. There was unusually strong Jesuit control and the proliferation of religious establishments was such that, by 1714, the clergy occupied three-quarters of the land in the city. By the end of the sixteenth century the city was ripe for great patronage of the arts, but no native painters of distinction were forthcoming. The first of the major new buildings, which is still the great museum of early Naples Baroque, the new Church of the Certosa of S. Martino, was begun in the 1580's in a Renaissance style, but it was taken over and remodelled by the young Cosimo Fanzaga, who arrived in Naples in 1608 and was to become the most employed architect and architectural impresario of the age. It is in the setting of Fanzaga's buildings that Neapolitan Baroque painting was created.

There is a sharp break in Neapolitan history, which is reflected in her art, in the year 1656. The plague of that year killed off two-thirds of the common people—and most of the first generation of painters who were still alive.

Although a number of painters in the Mannerist tradition continued working at Naples right into the 1630's, the brief passage of Caravaggio through Naples in 1606/7 may be said to have redirected Neapolitan painting along the line it was to follow for the first quarter of the century. Two of the altarpieces he painted during this year survive *in situ*. That in the Monte della Misericordia is an anthology of realistic motives rather oddly combined, but the *Flagellation* (fig.146) in S. Domenico Maggiore seems to anticipate and to dictate the taste of a whole generation. It is a fearsome scene in which brutal realism is redeemed by the classical balance of the design and the masterly modelling of the forms. The executioners are studied from the life and could be found in Naples today, but the result is a profoundly serious picture, of deep religious feeling, which accepts common nature as the medium through which divine truth is perceived—and rejects the ideal. This is sometimes thought to be a trait of Spanish art or of Spanish taste. Also a great deal of the picture is in darkness—and, although this was habitual with Caravaggio, it is only to his Neapolitan following that it has become customary to apply the term of 'tenebrist' or lover of darkness. It is a term only partially valid for Neapolitan painting, and only up to the 1630's.

146. CARAVAGGIO: *The Flagellation.* Naples, S.Domenico Maggiore

A single native painter, who may have been of Caravaggio's generation, perceived the new direction which Caravaggio's Neapolitan altarpieces had brought about and thus became the native founder of the Neapolitan school of the Seicento. This was Giovanni Battista Caracciolo (d. 1637), known as *Battistello*. Even the gentle

Caracciolo—and his best pictures are full of tender feeling—painted tenebrist pictures of *Salome* (Uffizi; fig.147) of a certain brutality. The revolution effected by Caravaggio is clear in his altarpieces in the Monte della Misericordia (1615) and the Pietà dei Turchini (1617), but there is at least stylistic evidence that he had visited Rome and studied the work of Annibale Carracci before he painted his master-piece, the *Washing of the Feet* of 1622 (fig.148) in the Certosa di S. Martino. In this picture, in which architecture gives a scale for the figures and the vivid red drapery of Christ marks him out from the subdued tones of the Apostles, whose individual psychology is studied with some attention, Battistello seems to anticipate what Poussin was later to make for himself from the rival sources of style available to him in Rome. It is already a break from the unredeemed tenebrism of his earlier work, and in his frescoes (the least damaged, of about 1631, are also in S. Martino), where he had no Caravaggesque models, he delights in a silvery light and pastel colours, which may represent more truly than his tenebrist works the natural bent of his genius. But by then he had been overshadowed as an influence by Ribera, and the frescoes of Lanfranco, who came to Naples in 1633, were to dominate the future of Neapolitan fresco painting.

147. BATTISTELLO: *Salome*. Florence, Uffizi

Detail from fig. 147

148. BATTISTELLO: *The Washing of the Feet*. Naples, S.Martino

149. STANZIONE: *The Deposition*. Naples, S.Martino

Next in age to Battistello was Massimo Stanzione (1585–1656), whose elegant art can be followed through a long series of datable altarpieces and frescoes. It reflects in turn Battistello, Ribera and Bolognese Classicism and can also be sufficiently seen in the Certosa of S. Martino. Only the *Deposition* (fig.149) of 1638, alleged to have been painted in some sort of competition with Ribera's 1637 picture of the same subject, shows real power and originality, and of an unexpectedly morbid kind. The bulk of Stanzione's work is merely respectable and he is most interesting as the master of Cavallino.

It was about 1616 that Jusepe Ribera (1591–1652), a native of Játiva, near Valencia, and nicknamed *lo Spagnoletto*, settled in Naples. Mancini, a contemporary, says that he had worked at Parma and made a considerable name for himself in Rome, in a Caravaggesque style, before he moved to Naples. Dated etchings, in a masterly style, begin in 1621, but we have no certain painting before 1626, when the artist was in his thirties and his personal style completely formed. His beginnings as a painter are still a complete mystery, but there can be little doubt that, although sometimes dull, all his certain works known to us speak with the authority of a great master. His style exactly hit the taste of Spanish Naples and he was Court painter to a succession of Viceroys, who sent or carried back to Spain a great number of his works, so that he is still most fully represented in the Prado in Madrid. But, though a Spaniard, he is an Italian painter with a Spanish accent and the dominant figure of the earlier Seicento at Naples and the only one with a truly European reputation. He introduced new themes into Italian painting and the bent of his taste can be paralleled by certain trends in Neapolitan literature of the time—not only Marino's doctrine that 'the purpose of art is to astonish', but Basile's interest in local folklore. Both are reflected in Ribera's use of common models as vehicles for religious expression. He painted best precisely what he had before his eyes.

Ribera first emerges as a painter of astonishing power in 1626 with *The drunken Silenus* (Naples, Gallery; fig.150), which may have been painted for the great Flemish merchant, Gaspar de Roomer, and certainly indicates, in its subject matter and treatment, some knowledge of Rubens and Van Dyck. Its technical mastery postulates many years of painting experience behind it, of whose fruits we have no knowledge. It is technically extremely original, with the form modelled and almost created by the sweeping strokes of a hard, coarse, brush. It is now—since the blue drapery has oxydized—almost without positive colour, simply sunburnt flesh seen against a dark ground and grey sky painted with the breadth of Daumier. By its authority and novelty it sweeps the timid works of Battistello and Stanzione aside and it is not surprising that, by 1638, Ribera had replaced them as the principal painter at the Certosa.

150. RIBERA: *Drunken Silenus*. Naples, Galleria Nazionale

151. RIBERA: *Jonah*. Naples, S.Martino

Between 1638 and 1643 he painted the series of over-lifesized *Prophets* in the
spandrels of the nave arcades (figs.151–2) in S. Martino which sum up a decade's
study of the weather-beaten models in whose form Ribera metaphorically descried
the Saints and Philosophers of old. It is instructive to compare their relation to real

152. RIBERA: *A Prophet*. Naples, S.Martino

life with that of Michelangelo's *Prophets* in the Sistine Chapel. Ribera's figures are certainly not common nature unadorned with reflective powers, but the sufferings which have made them what they are have been of a human and physical order. For Ribera human life was dignified in itself and did not need transfiguration—as it did

153. RIBERA: *Boy with a Clubfoot*. Paris, Louvre

for Michelangelo. This can be reinforced by considering one of the great master-pieces of seventeenth-century portraiture, Ribera's *Boy with a clubfoot* of 1642 (Paris, Louvre; fig.153). It is a commonplace to suggest that nothing else of the same order was painted until Manet: but its human values are conveyed with such penetrating sincerity that it makes Manet's pictures of this class look theatrical. The *Clubfooted boy*, with its unusually clear statement of the artist's attitude to-wards life—which is much less easy to read in his Beggar-Philosophers—serves as a touchstone by which we can interpret the whole of Ribera's art.

In the last decade of his life, parallel with the change of taste discernible in Rome during the 1640's, Ribera aimed increasingly at a noble tranquillity and figures of a more heroic or classical mould. His surface texture is much smoother than in his early work, his local colour is often strong, and, even when the background is dark, there is nothing left which can be called 'tenebrist'. A singularly tender and mellow

154. RIBERA: *The Marriage of S.Catherine.* New York, Metropolitan Museum

155. RIBERA: *The Communion of the Apostles*. Naples, S.Martino

example of this phase is the *Holy Family with S. Catherine* (fig.154) of 1648 in New York, but its masterpiece, too often decried, is the huge *Communion of the Apostles* (fig.155), finished in 1651, which was his last major painting and last work for the Certosa. It is one of the great works of Baroque Classicism and in the tradition of grave story-telling which goes back to Raphael's *Stanze*. The distant blue hills and the wide sky with fleecy clouds and a horde of clearly seen Bolognese cherubs are a far cry from Ribera's 'Caravaggesque' beginnings. The same sort of stylistic change was coming over the lesser Neapolitan painters of the time, but only Ribera shows the same authentic power in both idioms.

In the orbits of these three leading figures there worked half a dozen other painters, each of whom produced a few pictures of real distinction. The most interesting, at his rare best, was Francesco Fracanzano (1612–1656?), who married a sister of Salvator Rosa. In the two side paintings in the S. Gregory chapel in S. Gregorio Armeno (*S. Gregory consigned to the well*, c. 1635; fig.156) he shows a fine sense of drama and an original feeling for form as well as a liking for certain silvery tones which are also found in Salvator. The Roman Caravaggesque tradition was also reinforced by Artemisia Gentileschi, who worked in Naples for twenty years after 1630, and by Matthias Stomer, a Fleming who had developed in Rome a Caravaggesque style parallel with that of Honthorst. He seems to have been in Naples in the middle 1630's, where he had a certain influence on Cavallino, before moving on to fifteen years' work in Sicily. Rubens' huge *Salome* (Edinburgh) had reached the collection of Gaspar de Roomer in Naples, probably by 1640, and de Roomer was on intimate terms with all the painters of consequence, and his vast collection must have acted as a sort of Academy. Finally, two of the leading figures from the world of Roman painting were summoned to Naples for major decorative commissions, Domenichino for the Chapel of S. Gennaro in the Cathedral (inter-rupted activity at Naples from 1630 to 1641), and Lanfranco, who was in Naples from about 1633 to 1646 and left as his major work the frescoes in S. Martino.

So far we have only considered the great commissions for Church and Palace, but

156. F. FRACANZANO. *S.Gregory consigned to the Well*. Naples, S.Gregorio Armeno

the Neapolitan school was also remarkable for certain developments of painting on a more intimate scale.

It is refreshing to turn from the rather loud statement of the rest of Neapolitan painting to the tender wood-notes of Bernardo Cavallino (1616–1656?). Cavallino is never at his best in his few pictures on the scale of life: he preferred figures 'Poussin size', and his best works are all obviously private commissions and designed to appeal to the refined taste of discerning patrons, and to hang in their private Palaces. His art has a lyrical and feminine quality. It is, what is rare in Naples, the very opposite of vulgarity, and in expression and refinement it is clearly the work of a scrupulous and sophisticated mind. His refinement he perhaps derives from Battistello, his types from Stanzione, but there are amused overtones in the gestures and expressions of his figures which are far beyond Stanzione's powers. Most of his best work probably dates from the 1640's and early '50's, and it may be that the small pictures which suggest some Northern influence (such as the Tasso scenes at Munich) represent his earlier phase. A beautifully characteristic example is the *Esther and Ahasuerus* (Florence, Uffizi; fig.157), which has the shadowed silvery tone and sensitive colour effects which Cavallino loves undamaged. The story is dramatically treated with powerful and effective nuances, with very subtle expressions on the faces of the protagonists, even though they are in shadow. Caval-

157. CAVALLINO: *Esther and Ahasuerus*. Florence, Uffizi

158. CAVALLINO: *The Finding of Moses*. London, National Gallery

lino's art looks forward to the rococo, but it entirely lacks that shallowness of feeling which makes so much rococo painting cloying. His colouring is often extremely original. In the *Finding of Moses* (London, National Gallery; fig.158)—which may have been a little too much deprived of a certain final tone of mystery which I suspect Cavallino liked—the colours are brilliant and remarkable, ranging from a vivid lemon and blue-bag blue to the palest lilac and sage. They are used 'expressionistically', without concern for naturalism, as the violet hills and *marron* banks reveal, and the whole scene, a drama in which a lot of girls are involved, is extremely characteristic. There are a few lesser and more pedestrian figures, such as Hans Heinrich Schönfeld (1609–1682/83), who worked at Naples in the orbit of Cavallino, but, in the main, his art was too personal and too delicate to impose itself on others.

The other great individualist in the Neapolitan School was Salvator Rosa (1615–1673). He liked to think of himself as a Roman classic painter for the last thirty years of his life and he tried to forget his Neapolitan youth, but it is what he owed to Naples which made him the great forerunner of romantic landscape and one of the founding fathers of Romanticism. His *Self(?)portrait* (London, National Gallery; fig.159) tells us a good deal about him. He holds a placard which says 'Be silent, unless you have something to say which is better than Silence'—but he was never silent himself, and wrote a number of Satires on Art and Government which

159. SALVATOR ROSA: *Self(?)portrait.*
London, National Gallery

endeared him to nineteenth-century Liberals. His etchings—of which the most famous series, depicting studies of bandits and pirates, appeared in 1656—played perhaps the largest part in establishing that Salvator legend, which was summed up by the young Horace Walpole, who wrote, on crossing the Alps in 1739: 'Precipices, mountains, torrents, wolves, rumblings—Salvator Rosa'. Tradition indeed relates that his earliest pictures (which are totally unknown today) may have had something of this character. They were little studies of the wild mountain and coastal scenery of the Kingdom of Naples, populated by little figures of fishermen and bandits. One imagines them as a sort of Neapolitan anticipation of Guardi and the small

Bandits gambling (Rome, Galleria Nazionale; fig.160) may give some indication of what they were like. By 1639 he had left Naples for ever, to 'better himself', and passed by way of Rome to Tuscany, where he spent the years 1640–1649 in a learned and gay

society whichentirely altered his outlook on life. His *Seaports* and other pictures in the Pitti are all learnedly composed and, in the Satire on Painting he wrote during these years, he could state *Bisogna che i pittor siano eruditi* . . . ('Painters must be learned . . .'). From 1650 he worked in Rome, and the best of his later work is in fact a learned remodelling of his early Neapolitan material. The *Battlepiece* of 1652 (Paris, Louvre; fig.162), the last of a distinguished series, owes its origins to the Neapolitan Battlepieces of Aniello Falcone (1607–1656). It is a general *mêlée* without a particular theme or hero: but it has been given a heroic character by the study of Pietro da Cortona's *Battle of Issus* (fig.43), and the wild South-Italian land-

160. SALVATOR ROSA: *Bandits gambling.*
Rome, Galleria Nazionale

161. SALVATOR ROSA: *S.Onofrio*. Milan, Brera

scape and ruined temple make it a romantic landscape onto which a battle scene had
been superimposed. Indeed there is an area of dust or mist which separates the battle
from the landscape, as if they were independent, and it is the fact of Salvator's landscape backgrounds having an independent pictorial life of their own, with a novel kind
of picturesque sublimity, which endeared them to later generations. One can see this
very well in the *S. Onofrio* (Milan, Brera; fig.161) of the middle 1660's, which
originally balanced in S. Maria alla Vittoria a *S. John in the Wilderness* by Gaspard
Poussin (with the figure by Mola) (Milan, Brera; fig.57). Gaspard's wilderness is
park scenery, Salvator's has that wild character to which the eighteenth century
gave the attribute 'sublime'.

162. SALVATOR ROSA: *Battlepiece*. Paris, Louvre

163. SALVATOR ROSA: *The Death of Regulus*. Richmond, Va., Museum of Fine Arts

In the history pieces and Allegories of his Roman years Salvator, like Cavallino, is at his best when his figures are 'Poussin-size'. *The Death of Regulus* (Richmond, Va., Museum of Fine Arts; fig.163), perhaps of about 1650/52, is a savage master-piece of this style. In this too the bandit types of his early Neapolitan pictures have been reused and transmogrified into figures from classical history. However much he may have wanted to escape from his Neapolitan past, Salvator's strength lay in that original Neapolitan repertory which he had absorbed in his youth, and he can only properly be considered as one of the leaders of the Neapolitan school of paint-ing. Comparing his landscape with the Landscapes of Claude we see the antithesis of Naples versus Rome, of Romantic versus Classical. To the eighteenth century Salvator and Claude seem two commensurate and opposing giants. The style of both seemed equally familiar. The image of Claude we have today is still much the same as that which prevailed in the eighteenth century: but our image of Salvator has become much blurred by neglect and false attributions, and a great deal of research will be needed before we have a clear idea of what sort of an artist he really was.

The decimation of the painters who remained in Naples by the Plague of 1656 may have been the occasion for the arrival there of the Calabrian, Mattia Preti (1613–1699). It is with him that we arrive first at the Neapolitan High Baroque. His early training is obscure. He is thought to have gone to Rome about 1630 (probably by way of Naples) and it seems likely that he was largely influenced there by both the remainder of the Caravaggesque current and by the renewed interest in Venetian painting. Certainly he must at one time have made a study of Veronese. He was also impressed by Guercino's *Aurora* and by the grander frescoes of Domenichino. In 1650/51 he received the important commission to paint the frescoes in the apse of S. Andrea della Valle, where he had to compete with acknowledged masterpieces by both Lanfranco and Domenichino. The *S. Andrew bound to the Cross* (fig.164) shows remarkably powerful forms in the tradition of Domenichino, an extremely skilful organization of intricate groups, and a large general sweep of design which is already a long way towards the High Baroque. It was probably soon afterwards that he visited North Italy and painted the frescoes in the dome and apse of S. Biagio (Chiesa del Carmine) at Modena. These show an overwhelming dominance of the style of early Guercino, which was just what Preti needed to establish his personal style. This was ready by the time he reached Naples, where he painted two huge frescoes (now lost) in 1656/59, which were displayed over the Gate of Naples in commemoration of the Plague of 1656. The *modelli* for these survive in the Naples Gallery (fig.165) and are among the most splendid monuments of Neapolitan High Baroque, in which the learning of Venice, Bologna and Rome, and the 'Caravaggesque' idiom of the earlier Guercino have been fused together into a powerful and personal style—which was to remain constant for the rest of Preti's

164. PRETI: *S.Andrew bound to the Cross*. Rome, S.Andrea della Valle

long life. He made a short return to the Roman scene in 1661 when he painted in fresco *The Element of Air* (fig.166), one of his masterpieces, on the ceiling of a room in the Palazzo Doria-Pamphily at Valmontone, but soon afterwards he settled for good in Malta. At first he was engaged on the remodelling and decoration of the Cathedral of S. John at Valletta, but he later covered the whole island with a mass of his powerfully conceived and rapidly executed works. He also despatched from Malta a number of altarpieces to Naples and elsewhere.

165. PRETI: *Modello for the Plague Fresco*. Naples, Galleria Nazionale

166. PRETI: *The Element of Air*. Detail. Valmontone, Palazzo Doria

It may be that Preti was content to retire to Malta because of the emergence at Naples of another star, the young Luca Giordano (1634–1705). His execution was so rapid that he was known as 'fa presto' ('Do it quick'), and his output was so vast that new pictures are discovered each month. He begins as an infant prodigy well before the dividing year of 1656 and the first master whose style he absorbed was Ribera, and a good many early Giordanos still pass today under Ribera's name—though they are softer and have not quite Ribera's command of form or relentless gravity. Lanfranco's frescoes gave him an idea of what the High Baroque could be, and, at some date in the earlier '50's, Giordano went both to Rome and Venice, where he studied intensively chiefly Pietro da Cortona and Veronese. From Pietro he got a grasp of High Baroque principles, and from Veronese he got a feeling for a much higher key of colour than prevailed at Naples as well as a new repertory for the eloquent and graceful movement of human beings in dramatic action. He absorbed a good deal from any other old masters with whose work he came into contact, so that he could imitate or 'fake' anyone from Dürer or Rembrandt to Rubens and Bassano, for he had a gift of visual improvisation almost unsurpassed and a natural

167. GIORDANO: *The Deposition*. Venice, Accademia

feeling for Baroque swing and movement, which was unhampered by intellectual or theoretical complications. He could tell stories in paint with the easy naturalness of Veronese, but with the enhanced rhetoric of the High Baroque, and he gave proof of this in a series of altarpieces for Neapolitan Churches between 1655 and 1658. A fine example of his early style (certainly before 1659), in which Ribera still counts for a great deal, is the *Deposition* (fig.167) in the Venice Academy.

In a number of ways this remarkable picture anticipates the Venetian Rococo and

168. GIORDANO: *The Presentation in the Temple*. Venice, S.Maria della Salute

it had an immediate influence in Venice. Yet it looks back to Titian and to Veronese (especially in the *putti*). It is more passionate in feeling than most of Giordano's later works, but it reveals his personal idiom, made up of a combination of felicities which recall the work of other painters. Although Naples remained the main seat of his activities until he went to Spain in 1692, Giordano was a considerable traveller and his work rapidly acquired international renown. Venetian painting was revived by a series either of brief visits or of altarpieces which were sent there from the

169. GIORDANO: *Christ chasing the Merchants from the Temple.* Naples, Gerolomini

170. SOLIMENA: *Heliodorus expelled from the Temple*. Naples, Church of Gesù Nuovo

South. *The Presentation in the Temple* (Venice, S. Maria della Salute; fig.168), perhaps of the middle 1670's, was a restatement of a Venetian theme in terms of Roman Baroque which was profoundly influential: and Giordano's work at Florence in the 1680's has already been mentioned (p. 166 f.). He became capable of covering larger and larger spaces with his splendid *verve*, and the huge *Christ chasing the Merchants from the Temple*, 1684 (fig.169) on the entrance wall of the Gerolomini at Naples is only one of the most stupendous. The Neapolitan Viceroys were fascinated by his abilities and he was recommended to the King of Spain as the only man who could complete the pictorial decoration of the vast spaces of the Escorial within a measurable time.

From 1692 until 1702 he was in Spain, where he not only completed the Escorial frescoes, but did much work in the Churches of Madrid and for the Royal collection. Returning to Naples an old man, he achieved one of the airiest of his great undertakings in the ceiling of the Sacristy of the Certosa, completed in 1704, a little before his death—a model for the great decorative undertakings of the eighteenth century in Northern Europe.

Giordano's natural successor, and the last of the great figures of the Neapolitan Baroque, was Francesco Solimena (1657–1747). His training was not unlike Giordano's, but without benefit of Venice—but he made up for that by the study and admiration of Giordano's own work. At the height of his first mature period, 1689/90, when he painted the splendid frescoes in the Sacristy of S. Paolo Maggiore at Naples (*Fall of Simon Magus*: fig.171), he appears, in his gay colour and torrents of ingeniously arranged figures, to be simply a commensurate continuer of Giordano's art—with less genial facility, but greater intellectual elaboration of his designs. But during Giordano's absence in Spain a certain modification takes place in his art. He seems to have looked more and more to the dark shadows and high seriousness of Preti, and his pictures become increasingly dark, less busy. There are already signs, before a visit to Rome in 1700 and direct contact with Maratta, of a classical tendency in his compositions, and his figures take on a stately grandeur. Dr. Bologna has drawn attention to the parallel movement in literature, starting in Rome with the foundation of *Arcadia* in 1690, where there is also found a tendency towards simplification and an Anti-Baroque movement which was to develop into Neo-Classicism. In this context it is instructive to compare Solimena's huge *Heliodorus* (fig.170) of 1725 on the entrance wall of the Gesù Nuovo with its antagonist, Giordano's great fresco in the Gerolomini (fig.169). In the Giordano the movement is all *from* the centre, in the Solimena it all converges upon the central figure of the horseman. Solimena's space is a great amphitheatre, in which the action takes place: Giordano's is an illusionist stepped platform, seen from below, which provides the only stable opposition to a torrent of chaotic movement. Solimena's advance towards Neo-Classicism can be seen by considering the next stage, the *Pool of*

171. SOLIMENA: *The Fall of Simon Magus*. Naples, S.Paolo Maggiore

172. SOLIMENA: *Selfportrait*. Florence, Uffizi

Bethesda painted by his pupil Sebastiano Conca (1679–1764) in 1732 in the apse of S. Maria della Scala at Siena.

By the 1720's, though he never moved further from Naples than Rome, Solimena had become one of the great international painters and his works were sought in France, England and Germany. In 1730, after much negotiation, the Grand Duke of Tuscany succeeded in adding Solimena's *Selfportrait* (fig. 172) to the collection of portraits of artists in the Uffizi—a conscious Selfportrait of a Prince of Painters. In 1738 the young Alan Ramsay from distant Edinburgh spent some months in his studio, where he acquired a new feeling for grace which he introduced into British portraiture.

SICILY

THE pattern of painting in Sicily throughout the Seicento reflects what was happening in Naples, but painters of real distinction were extremely few. Caravaggio, in his brief passage through Sicily in 1608/9, left masterpieces at Palermo, Messina and Syracuse: but neither these nor the quite numerous altarpieces of the Flemish Caravaggista, Matthias Stomer, who worked in Sicily during the 1630's and 1640's, and whose masterpiece is the *S. Isidoro* (fig.173) of 1641 at Caccamo, inspired a native school worth mentioning. More important was the young Van Dyck's visit to

173. M. STOMER: *S.Isidoro.* Caccamo, S.Agostino

(199)

174. VAN DYCK: *Madonna of the Rosary*. Palermo, Oratorio del Rosario

175. NOVELLI: *S.Benedict blessing the loaves*. Monreale, Convento

Palermo for a few months in 1624. The plague forced him to cut short his visit, but he received commissions for two or three altarpieces for Palermitan churches, and these, especially that in the Oratorio del Rosario (fig.174), had a profound impression on the one native painter of real talent. This was Pietro Novelli (1603–1647), called *il Monrealese*. His average work could be mistaken for that of a Neapolitan of the second rank, but the huge painting of *S. Benedict blessing the loaves* (fig.175) of 1635, which hangs on the staircase of the former Convent attached to the Cathedral of Monreale, must rank as the masterpiece of Sicilian painting of the Seicento. Some of the figures have a courtly elegance of movement, which comes from Van Dyck, and this is accompanied by a tenderness of feeling, which is not to be found in Naples except in Cavallino. But this grand and noble picture is a solitary exception in what is otherwise something of a desert, and Sicilian painting of the second half of the century is of exceptional banality.

GENOA

AN independent school of painting is not to be traced at Genoa until after the establishment of the reformed Constitution in 1528, by which the Republic became a closed oligarchy, with all political power in the hands of two dozen noble 'families'. In spite of a series of conspiracies this constitution persisted throughout the whole Baroque period, and the arts profited by a situation in which a number of patrons of enormous wealth sought to outvie one another by the splendour of the Church or Palace with which each family was associated. The Ottoman domination in the East and the discovery of America had restricted Genoese trading interests to the Mediterranean and to Europe, which has led to the often-repeated judgment that Genoa was in decay during the seventeenth century. But the great Genoese trading families had in fact never been so prosperous, and the position of Genoa as the necessary port for Spanish Lombardy, and the stranglehold which the astute Genoese contrived to achieve over the immensely enriched but less businesslike economy of Spain make the period which runs from about 1560 to 1720 the golden age of Genoese art. In spite of the devastation of the last war Genoa can still show a series of Baroque Palaces, enriched with splendid frescoed apartments on the top floor, and retaining the remains of private picture collections, such as survive in no other Italian city. Unfortunately they are still among the least accessible treasures of Italian art. But a sufficient impression can be derived from the only ones open to the public, which

176. SINIBALDO SCORZA: *Landscape with Philemon and Baucis*. Edinburgh, National Gallery of Scotland

are the Palazzo Reale (formerly Durazzo), the Palazzo Rosso and the Palazzo Spinola in the Piazza di Pelliceria.

Since the close of the fifteenth century Genoa and the surrounding cities had been more sympathetic to the painting of the Netherlands than any other Italian centre. Flemish painters seemed to have been working there in the 1490's, and Genoese merchants in the Low Countries commissioned important works for Ligurian churches. The best view of Genoa of the period appears on a *Flora* of 1561 by Jan Matsys in the Stockholm Gallery. In the early seventeenth century a whole colony of Flemish painters was working in Genoa, which centred round the personalities of the brothers de Wael, who were hosts to Van Dyck on his first arrival there in 1621. An appetite for kitchen still-life pictures and landscapes with animal scenes can be traced among Genoese collectors at an early date, and the primacy for introducing this kind of painting into Italian art must go to Genoa. Its first Genoese master was Sinibaldo Scorza (1589–1631), whose *Landscape with Philemon and Baucis* (fig.176), with its companion, at Edinburgh, is a remarkably original and charming picture, which is among the first naturalistic, rustic, landscapes in the Flemish manner in Italian painting. It will be noted that the figures have a classical content. This tradition, reinforced by the parallel experiments of Jacopo Bassano and his descendants in the Veneto, accounts partly for the style of Castiglione, who was to be the most original Genoese painter of a later generation.

It is from the great masters of the Flemish school also that we are best introduced to the Genoese patrons of the Baroque age. Rubens painted a few members of the Genoese nobility about 1606, but it was Van Dyck who invented a new portrait formula, with social overtones of hitherto unexampled arrogance, for these gentlemen traders and their wives, who inhabited palaces of royal magnificence in princely state. For a few months in 1621/22 and later, after he had absorbed what Titian and the great Venetians had to teach him, for several years between 1623 and 1627, Van Dyck set up his studio in Genoa, and painted, as often as not, full lengths of great numbers of the local nobility. Those which survive in Genoa today are mostly in terrible condition, but it is not surprising that these splendid impositions should have appealed especially to British collectors of the Napoleonic age and later to the American millionaires. They can be most fully seen at the National Gallery in Washington today, but the *Marchesa Doria* in the Louvre (fig.177) gives the style to perfection. They are the most splendid portraits painted in Italy in the seventeenth century, but they did not really establish in Genoa a portrait tradition of comparable distinction. Except for a few portraits of Strozzi's Genoese years, no other portraits of the highest quality were produced in Genoa, and Van Dyck's principal native follower, Giovanni Bernardo Carbone (1614–1683), never rises beyond a pedestrian level. But Van Dyck's Venetianized style of painting counts a good deal, as we shall see, in the formation of some of the best of Genoese Baroque painters.

177. VAN DYCK: *Portrait of Marchesa Doria*. Paris, Louvre

It is with Bernardo Strozzi (1581–1644) that native Genoese Baroque begins. He was the best Genoese painter of the century, and, although his later work (after 1630) belongs to the history of Venetian painting (see pp. 125 ff.), his style was formed before he left for Venice, and its development cannot be understood without a glance at the Mannerist tradition in painting at Genoa during the sixteenth century.

The founder of the Genoese school was Luca Cambiaso (1527–1585). An admirable and original draughtsman, he had studied in Rome and also looked at

Venetian painting, and, at his best, he is more a Late Renaissance painter than a Mannerist. Not only did he initiate the Genoese tradition of historical fresco painting, he made experiments in 'nocturnes', which many modern scholars would have called 'Caravaggesque'—if only they had not been documented as having been painted before Caravaggio. But, after Cambiaso's death in Spain, there was no powerful personality in Genoa to carry on the tradition that he founded, and a number of lesser Mannerists from Central Italy were summoned to paint for Genoese churches. But a few more important pictures were commissioned from better painters, and Baroccio's splendid *Crucifixion* was hung in the Cathedral in 1596, while, probably soon after 1600, Francesco Vanni painted *The Last Communion of the Magdalen* (fig.179) for S. Maria Assunta di Carignano, and Ventura Salimbeni also received commissions for Genoa. Something of the style of these three painters is discernible in the earliest pictures of Bernardo Strozzi.

Strozzi seems to have had some training under a Tuscan Mannerist before he entered the Capuchin Order in 1597, but his career as a painter of consequence begins about 1610, when he was allowed out of the Cloister to practise his art to support his widowed and indigent mother. It is between 1610 and 1630, when he departed for Venice (perhaps under a religious cloud) that he formed his powerful and original style. Beginning perhaps as a religious painter, he early enlarged his repertory, and a picture such as *The Cook* (fig.178) in the Palazzo Rosso, reveals his

178. BERNARDO STROZZI: *The Cook*. Genoa, Palazzo Rosso

179. FRANCESCO VANNI: *The Last Communion of S.Mary Magdalen.*
Genoa, S.Maria di Carignano

awareness of the Flemish tradition of kitchen still-life painting, while certain groups of *Roistering peasants* suggest the work of an Italian equivalent of Jordaens.

His earliest style is admirably seen in the *S. Catherine* (fig.180) at Hartford. This

180. BERNARDO STROZZI: *S.Catherine*. Hartford, Conn., Wadsworth Atheneum

is hardly later than 1615 and is a skilful exercise in the Sienese Mannerist style, but with strange and original colour—luscious shades of white and cream and a cloak of a sort of mauve-magenta. The exaggerated oval of the face, with its blank but

181. BERNARDO STROZZI: *Pietà*. Genoa, Palazzo Bianco

devout expression, is echoed by a series of swinging curves which make few concessions to realism. But this style gradually gave way, between 1615 and 1620, to a greater naturalism, which shows an earnest desire to convey strong and precise feeling. The *Pietà* (fig.181; deposited by the Accademia Ligustica in the Palazzo Bianco, Genoa) shows this very effectively. The seductions of violent colour have been abandoned. Something of Mannerist grimace survives, but it is well on the way to being translated into a powerful vehicle for expressing emotion. There is great interest in the paint texture, which is tortured to look like clotted cream or icing sugar, and all possible edges are made interesting by broken contours.

To convert this promising manner into an original and mature style Strozzi turned to greater models: to Veronese, who was to become the idol of his Venetian years, and to Rubens, whose S. Ignatius altarpiece was set up in 1620 in the Gesù at Genoa. It was also in the early 1620's that the group of Flemish painters in the de Wael circle began to be most active in Genoa, and Strozzi's progress in the handling of paint suggests the attentive study of Flemish models. It is also possible that the appearance at Genoa in 1621 of Orazio Gentileschi (who painted at this time the *Annunciation* in S. Siro) may have counted for something in increasing in Strozzi an interest in powerful patterns in light and shade. In the *S. Augustine washing*

182. BERNARDO STROZZI: *S. Augustine washing Christ's Feet*. Genoa, Accademia Ligustica

183. ASSERETO: *S.Peter healing the lame Man*. Genoa, SS.Annunziata del Vastato

Christ's feet (fig.182; Accademia Ligustica, Genoa), a religious history beautifully and powerfully told, the mature Strozzi has emerged and he was ready to pass on to Venice and take up the inheritance of Veronese and Fetti.

One can show a line of descent from Strozzi for all the best Genoese painters of the succeeding century—except in the field of fresco painting, in which next to nothing of Strozzi's limited output has survived. But other painters of some distinction were developing at Genoa a style to some extent in parallel with that of Strozzi, but from a different tradition. The most interesting is Gioacchino Assereto (1600–1649), whose art is a child of the Lombard style of the Borromeo period, which had been transmitted to Genoa by G. C. Procaccini, who has left paintings in Genoa in SS. Annunziata del Vastato and S. Maria di Carignano. Except for the early *Circumcision* (Brera, Milan), Assereto's best canvases are not in public collections, but his surviving fresco of *S. Peter healing the lame man* (fig.183) in SS. Annunziata del Vastato reveals a painter of distinction among a mass of perfunctory fresco decoration. The date may be about 1640. There is no lack of frescoed ceiling decoration in Genoese churches of the period, but no sort of Baroque illusionism seems to have been attempted until the eighteenth century (S. Camillo). The painters who covered the largest areas (SS. Annunziata del Vastato, S. Siro, etc.) were the Carlone brothers, with or without *quadratura* schemes by other hands: but, though competently done, the quality of the single scenes does not encourage

184. VAN DYCK: *Ecce Homo*. Birmingham University, Barber Institute

the eye to linger upon their work. A good deal of gilding, often in high relief, is normal in Genoese church decoration, and SS. Annunziata del Vastato, before the damage caused by the last war, was one of the most profusely decorated churches in Italy.

The painter who at first followed most closely in Strozzi's footsteps was Giovanni Andrea de Ferrari (1598–1669), who began his independent practice about 1619. But he was soon profoundly affected by the work of Van Dyck, especially by that smooth elegance of surface and by that splendid distillation of Venetian style which can be seen in Van Dyck's later Genoese paintings—such as the *Ecce Homo* (fig.184) in the Barber Institute, Birmingham. In this there is a feeling for tone and texture which can make Strozzi seem coarse and ungraceful. Giovanni Andrea is at his best in the small biblical histories such as the *Esau selling his birthright* (fig.185: deposited by the Accademia Ligustica in the Palazzo Bianco) in which he could exhibit this feeling for tone and texture without overstraining his powers. This picture has Strozzi's colours but the refinement of Van Dyck, and it interprets the somewhat equivocal story with a poetic feeling for psychology. This quality can be faintly discerned in some of the many altarpieces which make up most of Giovanni Andrea's work, but he was not a great master of public expression and it is rather this poetic refinement and sensibility which he transmitted to two of his pupils, who were the best Genoese painters of the middle of the century—Valerio Castello (1624–1659) and Giovanni Benedetto Castiglione (1610—or earlier?—to 1665).

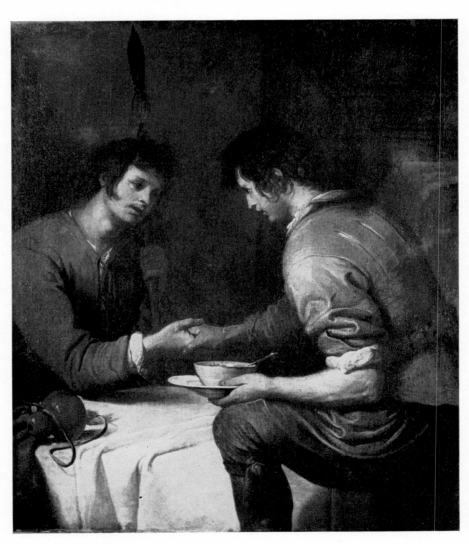

185. GIOVANNI ANDREA DE FERRARI: *Esau selling his birthright*. Genoa, Palazzo Bianco

186. VALERIO CASTELLO: *Allegory of Fame.* Genoa, Palazzo Reale

The short-lived Valerio Castello was the son of a rather conventional painter, Bernardo Castello, whose friendship with Tasso and Chiabrera, the most tenderly poetic spirits of his age, has preserved his name from merited oblivion. But Valerio was only five when his father died, and his natural inheritance—which should not be underestimated—was towards a poetic lyricism rather than a tradition of painting. This was reinforced by study under Giovanni Andrea de Ferrari, and even more by the experience of the work of Correggio at Parma. His latest pictures of domestic devotion, for which he is best known, are distillations of Correggiosity which look forward to the rococo in a way which is found, with much less charm, in the work of Nuvoloni at Milan. But his gifts were greater, both in fresco and history painting, than can be seen in the stock examples of his work. What must be his finest frescoes are in the inaccessible Palazzo Balbi di Piovera, but one can get an agreeable taste of his gifts as a fresco painter in a small room in the Palazzo Reale (fig.186) in which he has painted Fame on the ceiling and a series of Virtues (Loyalty, Gratitude and two others unidentified) in a rather heavy *quadratura* setting of rusticated arches by Giovanni Maria Mariani. There are also *putti* over the four doors of the room and

187. VALERIO CASTELLO: *S.Peter baptizing Saints James and John*. Genoa,
Oratorio di S.Giacomo della Marina

the rich colour and bold style of the figures marks them off from the perfunctory
and purely ornamental style of the other frescoes in the same Palace. This grand
style can be better seen in what is the masterpiece of his early maturity, the *S. Peter
baptizing SS. James and John* (fig.187) of 1646/47 in the Oratory of S. Giacomo della
Marina, a noble design blocked in with a bold pattern of light and shade, which
must once have had more resonant colour than it preserves today, though the group
with the woman at the lower right in honey-gold is still one of the most attractive
things in Genoese painting. Once one has gauged Castello's powers in this and the
Calling of S. James in the same Oratory, the rest of his work can be seen with understanding in the darker and more elusive corners of other Genoese churches in which
it is to be found. He was also the master of the 'modello', in a vivacious and almost

impressionist technique, which may well have been introduced to Genoa by Van Dyck. A rather more than usually finished example of these small studies is the *Marriage of the Virgin* (fig.188; Galleria Spinola, Genoa) in which the lightness and freshness of Castello's touch can be beautifully seen in the group at the lower left. This lively tradition he seems to have transmitted, by way of his dull pupil, Stefano Magnasco, to the latter's son, Alessandro Magnasco, whose eccentric work is the last flower of the Genoese Baroque style.

Castello's greater contemporary, Giovanni Benedetto Castiglione, stretches beyond the narrow confines of the Genoese school into a larger world. He was an enchanting etcher, he invented the monotype, and he has left behind (especially in the collection at Windsor) a series of 'drawings' in thin oil paint of the highest originality. In his graphic work he shows an awareness of the style of Rembrandt unique in Italy, but this can hardly be traced in his paintings. He seems to have begun in the Flemish-Genoese 'landscape with animals' style, which he sought to elevate by something of the Venetian colouring of the Bassano. The earliest pictures are astonishingly crowded with animals and pots and pans, and, even after he had

188. VALERIO CASTELLO: *The Marriage of the Virgin*. Genoa, Galleria Spinola

189. G. B. CASTIGLIONE: *The Angel appearing to the Shepherds*. Birmingham,
City Art Gallery

settled in Rome (at least by 1634), his predilection for subjects such as the Journeys
of the Patriarchs—which allowed for such *staffage*—was sufficiently notorious to
have become a joke. An excellent example is the *Angel appearing to the Shepherds*
(fig.189; City Art Gallery, Birmingham), which may be as late as 1640, in which a
traditional subject has been transformed to fit in with Castiglione's speciality. But
in this picture influences other than Genoese ones are strong, and the most powerful is that of one of the more romantic phases of Poussin's earlier style.

Positive information about Castiglione is extremely scarce, but there can be no
doubt that at Rome he was most closely associated with that group of artists who
were given a common centre by the Antiquarian studies of Cassiano dal Pozzo. The
most powerful artistic personality among them was Poussin, but the painter whose
temperament was most akin to that of Castiglione was Pietro Testa. In this climate
Castiglione added romantic and mythological subjects to his repertory. Although he
can be traced in Rome as late as 1650, he seems to have been at least equally based
on Genoa, for several large religious paintings were made for the Genoa
region and in the 1640's. The finest is the *Nativity* (fig.190) of 1645 in S. Luca,
Genoa, a lovely invention in which the slightly bizarre figures of Castiglione's
Roman pastorals are romantically blended with the religious theme and produce a
poetic result very different from the common run of Baroque Nativities. Soon afterwards, about 1646/47, he painted the *St. James driving the Moors from Spain*

190. G. B. CASTIGLIONE: *The Nativity*. Genoa, S.Luca

191. G. B. CASTIGLIONE: *S.James driving the Moors from Spain*. Genoa,
Oratorio di S.Giacomo della Marina

in the Oratory of S. Giacomo della Marina (fig.191), which shows an unexpected
study of Rubens and a hardly less surprising power for painting dramatic histories
on the scale of life. For most of the time after 1650 he was attached to the Court at
Mantua—though what work he did for the Court is obscure—but he continued to
maintain his links with Genoa. What is presumably his later style is well represented
by the brilliant and passionate *Crucifixion* (fig.192; Palazzo Bianco, Genoa) which is
closer to his late monotypes and work as a draughtsman than any other of his
paintings. As with Castello's 'modelli', this seems to look forward to the style of
Magnasco.

The Oratory of S. Giacomo della Marina (which can only conveniently be seen
on a Sunday morning) has already been mentioned as containing two of the most

192. G. B. CASTIGLIONE: *The Crucifixion*. Genoa, Palazzo Bianco

remarkable of Genoese pictures: and the large stories from the life of S. James which decorate the side walls and were all painted about 1646/47 include the master-pieces of other Genoese artists. One of them is G. B. Carlone's masterpiece, and another is the earliest and perhaps best picture of the leading figure of the next generation, Domenico Piola (1627–1703). This is the *Martyrdom and Ascension of S. James* (fig.193) dated 1647, which is a distinguished variation of the style of the older painters whose work Piola could see around him. For the next thirty years Piola painted an endless number of altarpieces and frescoes for Ligurian churches which call for no comment, but he seems to have received a new inspiration with the appearance of Gregorio de Ferrari (1647–1726), who became his assistant about

193. DOMENICO PIOLA: *The Martyrdom and Ascension of S.James*. Genoa,
Oratorio di S.Giacomo della Marina

1673 and his son-in-law the following year. About this date each painted one of the
domes in the South aisle of S. Siro with an agreeable Correggiesque bravura, and a
number of Piola's later studies (of which there are very many in the Palazzo Bianco)
have this lively quality.

It was in fact the direct experience of Correggio's work at Parma, where he
studied for a few years before 1673, that made Gregorio de Ferrari the last considerable exponent of the Grand Style in Genoa and the first master of the Genoese
rococo. It is reflected most unequivocally in the early *Rest on the Flight* (fig.194),
painted for the Theatines of Sampierdarena but now rather skied in the Sacristy of
S. Siro, Genoa. The S. Joseph in almost pastel shades of soft blue, rose and orange
is cribbed straight from Correggio and so is the tender mood and lyrical quality of

194. GREGORIO DE FERRARI: *The Rest on the Flight into Egypt*. Genoa, S.Siro

195. GREGORIO DE FERRARI: *Cupid and Psyche*. Genoa, Palazzo Granello

the presentation. Soon he was to transfer these qualities to large fresco series, of which the most accessible are what remains in the Palazzo Rosso (1692). But these are eclipsed in rococo airiness by the *Cupid and Psyche* ceiling (fig.195) of a year or two later in the rather inaccessible Palazzo Saluzzo-Granello in the retired Piazza dei Giustiniani. Here he almost anticipates Fragonard. In his latest work, of after 1700, he not only achieved such a rococo interpretation of late Bernini as the *Death of S. Scolastica* in S. Stefano, but he was responsible for the first Genoese Church ceiling and dome decoration which was really conceived as a unitary scheme. This is the small church of S. Camillo de Lellis (S. Croce) painted 1715/20 with the help of his son Lorenzo (1680–1744). Here there is a crinkly octagonal dome, with crinkly spandrels, which, together with the ceiling of the nave of a single bay, are painted as a single unit of decoration in fresco and gilt.

The last eminent figure among Genoese Baroque painters is an artist of very different tendency, whose public commissions barely exist, and whose *forte* was the brilliant improvisation (often in collaboration with obscure painters of architecture or landscape) of small scenes of picaresque genre and religious asceticism for private collectors. Alessandro Magnasco (1667–1749), often called *il Lissandrino*, spent most of his working life at Milan (with a year or two in Florence) and only returned to Genoa in 1735, where his art does not seem to have been much liked. But though he is recorded as having been trained by an obscure Milanese painter, the roots of his style, a nervous calligraphic style of flicks, which is altogether unapt for the rendering of anything but a neurotic world, go back to Genoa, to the *bozzetti* of Valerio Castello, and to the late drawings and studies of Castiglione (such as the *Crucifixicn*, fig.192). The moral content of Magnasco's pictures is obscure. Is the behaviour of his friars mystically devout or laughably absurd? Is he a covert critic, within a world of ecclesiastical censorship, of a religiosity which had got out of hand? It is not an accident that he was a contemporary of Watteau, whose world is ambiguous in a manner infinitely more refined, and that both Magnasco and Watteau owe a good deal to a predecessor of a somewhat satiric character—Magnasco to Callot, Watteau to Gillot. It is also perhaps relevant that the other figures in Magnasco's works are mainly figures from low life, brigands, mountebanks and the like. His production was enormous and his 'form' sufficiently consistent to make stylistic dating impossible. A word should be said about his stormy seas, which achieve a turbulence far beyond the possibilities even of the theatre. Even Magnasco's tormented puppets cannot quite live up to the violence which he attributes to the forces of nature. Of this style there are two excellent examples in the Castello Sforzesco at Milan (fig.196). But a more impressive picture is the scene in the Poldi-Pezzoli, Milan (fig.198), which is called '*S. Charles Borromeo receiving oblates*'. The central figure is certainly a Cardinal and has some likeness to S. Charles: but the scene is visionary and not of this world. The Baroque figures adorning a Classic temple have come to life (as garden statuary sometimes does in Watteau), and the scene has the air of some act of penitence or absolution being enacted in extreme

196. MAGNASCO: *Friars and a stormy sea*. Milan, Castello Sforzesco

197. MAGNASCO: *Figures on a Terrace at Albaro*. Genoa, Palazzo Bianco

198. MAGNASCO: *A Cardinal receiving Friars*. Milan, Museo Poldi-Pezzoli

urgency before a final cataclysm. In the large *Figures on a terrace at Albaro* (fig.197;
Palazzo Bianco, Genoa) which, though uncharacteristic, is perhaps his masterpiece
and may date from his last Genoese years, the parallel with Watteau is closer—but
those human values which make Watteau's figures so poignant have been drained
out of Magnasco's puppets, and we are looking at the end of an ugly world rather
than at the budding promise of a new Arcadia.

BIBLIOGRAPHICAL NOTE

INDEX OF PLACES

INDEX OF NAMES

BIBLIOGRAPHICAL NOTE

THE two fullest and best bibliographies, which cover all the arts in Italy during the seventeenth and eighteenth centuries, are in Vincenzo Golzio, *Seicento e Settecento*, 2nd edition, 2 vols. Turin, 1961: and in Rudolf Wittkower's volume in the Pelican History of Art, *Art and Architecture in Italy 1600 to 1750*, 1965. Since this latter volume will be accessible to anyone interested in pursuing this subject further (they would be well advised to own it) I have listed below only one or two essential titles and such articles as I have actually referred to in the text, and such articles as have appeared since 1958 that I have found useful for factual information. Very full bibliographies are also to be found in the catalogues of the following Exhibitions which have been held in recent years:

Caravaggio e Caravaggeschi, Milan, 1951.

Cigoli e suo ambiente, S. Miniato al Tedesco, 1959.

Pittori genovesi del seicento e del settecento, Genoa, 1938.

Seicento e settecento in Liguria, Genoa, 1947.

Pittori della realta in Lombardia, Milan, 1953.

Manierismo piemontese e lombardo del seicento, Turin, 1955.

Seicento emiliano, Bologna, 1959.

Seicento Europeo, Rome, 1957.

Il settecento a Roma, Rome, 1959.

Seicento Veneziano, Venice, 1959.

The forthcoming revised edition of Hermann Voss, *Die Malerei des Barock in Rome* (1924) will be the fullest book on the central theme of Italian Baroque painting.

Addenda to Wittkower and essential books, alphabetically under artists:

BADALOCCHIO. L. Salerno in *Commentari*, 1958, 44 ff.

BAMBOCCIO etc. *I Bamboccianti* by G. Briganti, Rome, 1950.

BAROCCIO. Harald Olsen, *Federico Barocci*, Stockholm, 1955.

CARAVAGGIO. Walter Friedlaender, *Caravaggio Studies*, Princeton, 1955. Mary Anne Graeve (on the *Deposition*) *Art Bulletin*, 1958, 223. Leo Steinberg (on the Cerasi Chapel) *Art Bulletin*, 1959, 183.

CARRACCI. Mostra dei Carracci, Catalogue, Bologna, 1956. J. R. Martin (on the Camerino Farnese) *Art Bulletin*, 1956.

CIGOLI. Mostra del Cigoli etc. San Miniato, 1959.

CORTONA. P. da. Mostra di P. da Cortona, Rome, 1956: Giuliano Briganti, *Pietro da Cortona*, Florence, 1962.

DOLCI. G. Heinz, Vienna *Jahrbuch* 56 (xx), 1960, pp. 197 ff.

DOMENICHINO. Alberto Neppi. *Gli affreschi del D. a Roma*, Rome, 1958.

DUGHET. Gaspard. Denys Sutton in *Gazette des Beaux-Arts*, 1962.

D. FETTI. Pamela Askew, The Parable paintings, in *Art Bulletin*, 1961.

O. GENTILESCHI. Charles Sterling in *Burlington Magazine*, April 1958.

F. GHERARDI. A. M. Cerrato in *Commentari*, 1959, 159 ff.

LANFRANCO. Luigi Salerno in *Commentari*, 1958, 44 ff. & 216 ff.

MARATTA. Anna Mezzetti in *Rivista dell' Istituto Nazionale d'Archeologia e Storia dell' Arte*, 1955.

MOLA. Lina Montalto in *Commentari*, 1955, 267 ff.

FRATEL' POZZO. Remigio Marini, *Andrea Pozzo*, Trento, 1959.

PRETI. Claudia Refice, *Mattia Preti*, Brindisi, [1961].

GUIDO RENI. Mostra di Guido Reni, Bologna, 1954. C. Gnudi & G. C. Cavalli, *Guido Reni*, Florence, 1955.

SANTI DI TITO. Gunter Arnolds, *Santi di Tito*, Arezzo, 1934.

SARACENI. Valerio Martinelli in *Studi Romani*, 1959.

SOLIMENA. F. Bologna, *Francesco Solimena*, Naples, 1958.

STOMER. H. Pauwels in *Gentse Bijdragen*, 1953.

TANZIO DA VARALLO. Mostra di Tanzio da Varallo, Turin, 1959/60.

LE VALENTIN. R. Longhi in *Revue des Arts*, 1958, 58 ff.

Further Addenda, 1968

BACICCIA. Robert Enggass, *Baciccio*, University Park, Pa., 1964.

CAGNACCI. Mario Zuffa in *Arte antica e moderna* 1963, pp. 357 ff.

CASTIGLIONE. Ann Percy in *Burl. Mag.*, Dec. 1967. 672 ff.

DOMENICHINO. Evelina Borea. *Domenichino*. Milan 1965.

GIORDANO. Oreste Ferrari & Giuseppe Scavizzi. *Luca Giordano*, 3 vols., 1966.

There is a useful bibliographical note in the Addenda, vol. II, pp. 135-6, to Alfred Moir, *The Italian Followers of Caravaggio*, 2 vols., Harvard 1967.

INDEX OF PLACES

INDEX OF NAMES

Date Due

MAR 15 1971				
OCT 1 9 1974				
DEC 1 6 1974				
MAR 2 4 1975				